Science Fair Success

Science Fair Success Using Supermarket Products

Salvatore Tocci

Enslow Publishers, Inc.

40 Industrial Road   PO Box 38
Box 398   Aldershot
Berkeley Heights, NJ 07922   Hants GU12 6BP
USA   UK

http://www.enslow.com

Library of Congress Cataloging-in-Publication Data

Tocci, Salvatore.
    Science fair success using supermarket products / Salvatore Tocci.
       p. cm. — (Science fair success)
    Includes bibliographical references and index.
    Summary: Presents chemistry projects and experiments that can be done using
supermarket products.
    ISBN 0-7660-1288-3
    1. Food—Experiments Juvenile literature. 2. Science—Experiments
Juvenile literature. [1. Food—Experiments. 2. Science—Experiments.
3. Experiments.]   I. Title. II. Series.
TX355.T63   2000
507'.8—DC21   99-26193
                                            CIP

Printed in the United States of America

10 9 8 7 6 5 4 3 2

To Our Readers:
All Internet addresses in this book were active and appropriate when we went to press. Any
comments or suggestions can be sent by e-mail to Comments@enslow.com or to the address on
the back cover.

Illustration Credits: Stephen F. Delisle

Photo Credits: Enslow Publishers, Inc.

Cover Photo: © TSM/Jose L. Pelaez

Contents

Introduction.   5

1 Beverages   11

  1.1 What Can Happen When Water Freezes?   13

  1.2 How Cold Can It Get?   18

  1.3 How Can You Concentrate a Solution?.   22

  1.4 How Can You Keep Fruits and Salads Fresh? . .   24

  1.5 How Much Vitamin C Does
     Orange Juice Contain?   26

  1.6 How Can You Get Rid of a Solute?.   29

  1.7 How Does Temperature Affect Dissolving?   30

2 Dairy Products. .32

  2.1 How Can You Turn Milk into Cheese? 34

  2.2 What Is the Mineral Content of Milk?   38

  2.3 What Is the Protein Content of Milk?.   41

  2.4 Can You Measure How Unsaturated a Fat Is? . .   46

  2.5 How Did Your Great-Grandmother
     Make Butter?.   51

  2.6 How Can You Mix Oil and Vinegar?   53

3 Fruits and Vegetables.   55

  3.1 Have You Ever Used Fruits or Vegetables to
     Decorate a Cake?.   56

  3.2 Is It an Acid or a Base?   59

  3.3 What Is the pH of Rain?.   62

3.4 Which Color(s) Do Plants Prefer
for Photosynthesis? 64

3.5 Is Green the Only Pigment in Plants? 67

3.6 Why Do Plants Wilt? 71

3.7 What Is Inside a Seed?. 74

3.8 Why Is Making a Pineapple Gelatin Dessert
Not a Good Idea? 77

4 Meat Products 79

4.1 What Can You Do with Liver Besides Eat It? . . 80

4.2 How Do You Soften a Tough Piece of Beef? . . . 85

4.3 Where's the Beef? 86

4.4 Why Do Bones Sometimes Break So Easily? . . . 92

5 Snacks, Desserts, and Candies 98

5.1 How Many Calories Does One Potato
Chip Contain?. 100

5.2 What Makes Popcorn Pop? 105

5.3 How Can You Make Popcorn "Dance"? 107

5.4 How Much Sugar Does a Cookie Contain?. . . . 109

5.5 How Much Sugar Does Gum Contain?. 111

5.6 What Is Rock Candy? 112

5.7 How Many Colors Are Really Present
in a Candy?. 116

Glossary 119

Further Reading 123

List of Suppliers. 125

Index 127

Introduction

How many times have you been told by an adult not to play with your food at the dinner table? Well, this book gives you the chance to "play" with your food any time you want without getting in trouble. In fact, adults will probably be very pleased to see you "playing" with your food. But, as they will have discovered, you will not actually be playing. Rather, you will be carrying out experiments on an assortment of products that are sold in a supermarket, including various foods and beverages.

As you progress through this book, you will first be given some information about the science behind a particular supermarket product. Then, you will be shown how to carry out an experiment with that product. At the end of some experiments, you will find an idea for a science project that is related to the product. You will be given enough information to start the project. However, you will have to do some research to get additional information that you will probably need to finish the project. You can use your school or local library, check with your science teacher, or search the Internet. Some ideas for projects will involve products that you may not find in a supermarket but can locate either at home or in a local store.

All the products needed for the experiments in this book,

however, are likely to be found right in your kitchen. Whatever you do not have at home can be bought in a local supermarket. But you will not have to shop for any laboratory equipment or supplies to carry out your experiments. All the experiments described in this book can be done at home, using common household appliances, utensils, and assorted ordinary items.

To convince any skeptical adults of the value of "playing" with food, point out that foods and beverages are nothing more than chemicals. If you look up the word *chemical* in a dictionary, you will see it defined as "a substance produced or used in a chemical process." This definition, however, probably does not really help you understand what a chemical is.

To get a better idea of what a chemical is, pour yourself a glass of tap water. Picture yourself peering into the water with the most powerful microscope in the world. What you would see would be individual particles of water. You would also see other particles besides those of water. Each type of particle is a different chemical. Scientists give each chemical both a name and a formula. For example, one of the chemicals you would see is water, whose formula is H_2O. The actual chemical name for water is dihydrogen oxide. This name indicates that water is made up of two hydrogen atoms and one oxygen atom. An **atom** is the basic unit of a chemical. Besides water, another chemical you would see is ordinary table salt. The chemical name for table salt is sodium chloride and its formula is NaCl. You will work with H_2O, NaCl, and other chemicals as you carry out the experiments in this book.

Keep in mind that this book is only an introduction to experiments and projects that you can perform with foods and beverages. Do not be limited by what is written here. Use what you learn and your imagination to come up with ideas for additional experiments and projects. Perhaps something you do with a particular food product in one chapter can be used with a different product mentioned in another chapter. Also, do not be afraid to vary the procedures that are given. For example, if the procedure calls for seeing what happens when you heat something, you may want to experiment a little further. You can check to see whether there is a difference between heating gently and heating strongly. Or you may want to find out whether cooling has the same effect. Always seek the advice of an adult when designing your own experiment.

Include a Control

If you decide to follow up one of the suggestions for a project described in this book, be sure you know what to do if your procedure involves designing an experiment. Many experiments require a control. This does not mean that the person has total control over what is going into the experiment. Rather, a control allows the experimenter to design the procedure so that what happens can likely be explained. Consider a simple experiment. Assume that you drop a chemical into a blue-colored liquid. The liquid turns yellow. You conclude that the chemical caused the liquid to change color, which is a valid assumption. However, someone could argue that the liquid changed color for another reason. Perhaps the light, temperature, or air in the room was responsible for the change in color. Although these causes seem unlikely, they might be responsible for what happened.

A better design for this experiment would involve two

Chapter 1

Beverages

You can find an assortment of beverages in your home, including milk, coffee, tea, juices, and sodas. Each of these, in turn, comes in a wide variety. For example, the milk container in your refrigerator may be labeled *nonfat*, *1% fat*, *2% fat*, *whole*, or *buttermilk*. The soda can in your kitchen cabinet may be labeled *diet* or *caffeine free*. No matter what beverages they are, however, they have one thing in common—they all contain water.

Water Is an Unusual Chemical

Water is easily taken for granted. After all, water is always available by just turning on a faucet. Water also seems so ordinary. It has no color, taste, or odor. But despite its ordinary characteristics, water is no ordinary chemical. In fact, water is one of the most unusual chemicals known to scientists. For example, water is one of the very few chemicals that can simultaneously exist in nature in three different forms. Depending on the temperature, water can be a solid (snow or ice), a liquid (rain), or a gas (vapor). Increasing the temperature will turn the solid into a liquid. This is what happens to snow when it gets warmer. If the temperature continues to increase, then the liquid will turn into a vapor. Think about what happens when heat from the sun evaporates the rain that has fallen.

Experiment 1.1

What Can Happen When Water Freezes?

Materials

* empty plastic milk container with lid
* freezer
* water

Something unusual occurs when the temperature gets cold enough to change water from a liquid to a solid. At first as the temperature drops, the particles of water behave like those of other liquids by moving closer to one another. But then as the temperature of the water approaches the freezing point, the particles do something unusual. Rather than continuing to move even closer, the particles of water begin to move farther and farther apart. As a result, the water particles as a solid take up more space than they did as a liquid. This is a simple experiment to prove that water takes up more space after it freezes.

Completely fill an empty plastic milk container to the brim with water. Securely tighten the lid, making sure that no air bubbles have been trapped inside the container. If they have, remove the top and add the water slowly to bring the level of the water to the very top of the container. Place the sealed container in a freezer for at least twenty-four hours. If the milk container is too large to fit in the freezer, you can use an empty pill or vitamin container to fill with water.

Carefully examine the container and notice what happened. Does your container look like the one shown in Figure 1? If so, the container expanded because the particles moved apart when the liquid turned into a solid. Because there was no space left inside the container, the particles "pushed" on the plastic, causing it to expand or bulge. If your container did not expand, check to make sure your freezer is working properly!

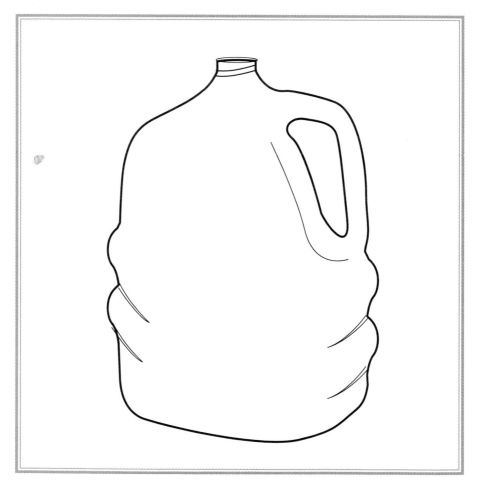

Figure 1. As ice formed inside this container, the water particles took up more space than they did as a liquid. Because they had nowhere else to go, these water particles pushed out the sides of the container.

Project Idea

Building a Model

Perhaps you have built a model car, airplane, train, or boat. If you have, then you realize that building models is not only fun but also helpful in understanding how the device operates. Scientists also build models. The models take many forms, from replicas to written descriptions. When building a model, scientists base the construction on the information or data they have collected. The model might then help them understand what is happening. Moreover, the model can enable scientists to make predictions. Consider how scientists use models in studying weather patterns.

A meteorologist, or scientist who studies the weather, may assemble a lot of information to make a computer model of weather patterns. The model not only shows the current weather conditions in different areas, but also forecasts the weather over the next few days. By the way, did you ever notice that meteorologists never predict but only forecast the weather? What is the difference? While you are thinking about the answer, also consider constructing a model to show what happens when water freezes.

For example, you might use a computer drawing program to construct a model that shows how water particles behave as the user changes the temperature. Or you can construct a model using a supermarket product, such as canned or frozen peas, to represent the water particles. Whatever type of model you construct, be sure that it includes the solid, liquid, and vapor forms of water. Check with a physical science or chemistry teacher for more detailed information about water and what happens as the temperature changes. Also check your school library or search the Internet for information about other unusual properties of water that you might include as part of your project. Key phrases to use in your search are "heat capacity of water" and "attractive forces in water."

As part of your project, include information about what happens to the density of water as it changes between a solid, liquid, and vapor. **Density** is defined as the quantity of mass present in a given volume. The more mass in a given volume, the denser the substance. Ice is less dense than water. Thus ice floats on water. Based on what happened to the container in Figure 1, can you explain why ice is less dense than water? How would life in ponds, lakes, and other bodies of water be affected if ice were denser than water?

Freezing and Boiling Points

The temperature at which liquid water turns into a solid was important in developing the thermometer scale used in science laboratories today. In the eighteenth century, a Swedish scientist, Anders Celsius, placed an unmarked thermometer in water that he first cooled and then heated. The point on the thermometer where ice started to form is the freezing point. The freezing point of water was set at 0° Celsius (C). The point on the thermometer where vapor started to form is the boiling point. The boiling point of water was set at 100°C.

In the United States, a thermometer that is used to measure your body temperature will not be marked in the Celsius scale but rather in the Fahrenheit scale. The Fahrenheit system is older than the Celsius scale. But in this case, you do not have to respect age. In fact, scientists throughout the world prefer the younger, Celsius scale. There is another scale they often use—the Kelvin scale. On the Kelvin scale, 0° is known as "absolute zero" where all atoms would cease to move. The atoms that make up a liquid or gas move freely. In contrast, atoms in a solid remain in a fixed position, but they still vibrate back and forth. However, at absolute zero, atoms would neither move nor vibrate. Scientists have come close in their attempts to achieve absolute zero but have not quite made it.

One way to avoid all this confusion about scales is to use an indoor/outdoor thermometer. As you can see in Figure 2, this type of thermometer is usually marked in both the Celsius and Fahrenheit scales. Having both scales on the same thermometer makes life easy because you can quickly convert from one scale to the other. For example, normal human body temperature is 98.6°F. If you check an indoor/outdoor thermometer that has both scales, you will see that this corresponds to 37°C. The following equation shows you how to convert from °F to °C.

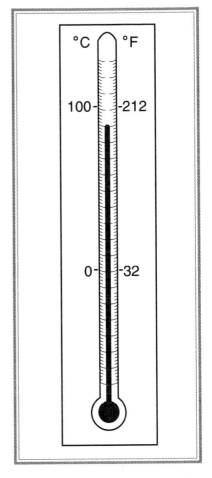

Figure 2. The boiling point of water is 100° on the Celsius scale and 212° on the Fahrenheit scale. Scientists throughout the world use the Celsius scale because, like other metric units, it is based on multiples of 10.

$$°C = \frac{5}{9} \times (°F - 32)$$

Experiment 1.2

How Cold Can It Get?

On a cold February morning on your way to school, you have probably learned something about nature—the air temperature does go below freezing. This refers, of course, to the freezing point of water—0°C, or 32°F. But can the temperature of water go below freezing? Here is an experiment you can do to find out.

Crush about fourteen ice cubes by wrapping them in a towel and gently hitting them with a hammer. Be sure to crush the ice outdoors and not on the kitchen countertop. Add

Materials

* large Styrofoam cup
* empty plastic pill container
* tray of ice cubes
* hammer
* towel
* rock, coarse, or table salt
* tablespoon
* water
* indoor/outdoor thermometer

the crushed ice to nearly fill a Styrofoam cup. Then add five tablespoons of salt to the crushed ice and mix. Place an empty pill container in the cup. Pour some water into the container. Make sure that the level of the ice-salt mixture is above the level of the water in the pill container, as shown in Figure 3.

Watch the water in the container to see when ice starts to form. At this point, place an indoor/outdoor thermometer in the ice-salt mixture. How low does the temperature go? You should now be able to explain why salt is sometimes spread on icy roads. But in many areas salt has been replaced by sand. Do you know why?

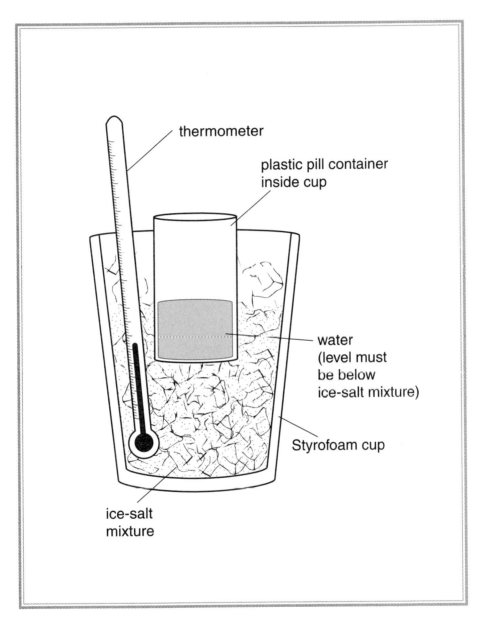

Figure 3. When ice starts to form inside the pill container, place a thermometer in the ice-salt mixture in the Styrofoam cup. Why must the level of the water in the pill container be below that of the ice in the Styrofoam cup? By the way, why is a Styrofoam cup used?

Colligative Property

Here is your chance to impress your friends the next time they shake some salt on their food. Simply shake some salt into a cup of water. When your friends ask what you are doing, tell them that you are investigating a colligative property. But before you do this, be sure you know what this term means. The word *property* refers to an attribute or a trait that something has. For example, the freezing point of water is a property of water. A colligative property is a property that depends on only one thing—the number of particles that are present. A **colligative property** does not depend on the size or weight of those particles, just on how many are present. Consider what happens to the freezing point of water—a colligative property—when something else is added to the water.

For example, adding salt to water lowers its freezing point. The more salt added, the lower the freezing point. But it does not matter what you add as long as the number of particles is the same in every case. For example, the freezing point of water will be lowered to the same extent if you add salt or sugar, as long as they both completely dissolve in the water to produce an equal number of particles. In fact, if you dissolve the same number of sugar or salt particles in water, its boiling point will be raised to the same extent.

Project Idea

Constructing an Ice Cream Maker

Colligative properties are the basis for making ice cream. Salt is added to ice to achieve the cold temperature that is needed. If you do not have an ice cream maker, Figure 4 shows how you can make a really simple one from items that you can find at home. You could also clean an empty metal coffee can for mixing the ingredients. This can be placed inside a larger one that contains the mixture of salt and ice. You can stir the ingredients by hand or use an electric mixer. Experiment by trying different recipes.

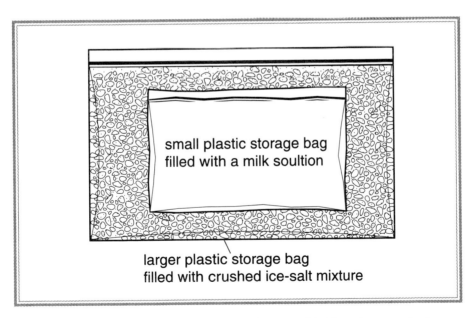

small plastic storage bag
filled with a milk soultion

larger plastic storage bag
filled with crushed ice-salt mixture

Figure 4. A simple ice cream maker can be assembled by using two plastic food-storage bags. A smaller one is placed inside the larger one. The smaller one contains the ingredients needed for making the ice cream. The larger one contains an ice-salt mixture needed to maintain the cold temperature.

Experiment 1.3

How Can You Concentrate a Solution?

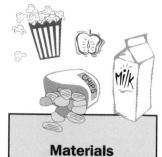

Water is used to dissolve many different substances. Perhaps you like to drink iced tea in the summer. You fill a glass with water and ice, add some powdered tea, pour in some sugar, squeeze in a little lemon juice, and stir. Stirring causes the particles to dissolve in the water until they are too small to see.

Whenever you have dissolved something in water so that you can no longer see it, you have made a **solution**. Water can dissolve many different substances to form solutions. The water is known as a **solvent**. A solvent is the substance that does the dissolving. The substance that is dissolved—the powdered tea or sugar—is called the **solute**. Together, the solvent and solute make a solution. Most of the beverages in your home are solutions.

Solutions can be dilute, concentrated, or somewhere in between. It all depends on how many solutes are present. Think of dilute and concentrated solutions in this way. You decide to have a sleep-over party at your house. At first, you invite just one friend. Thus, there would be two of you sleeping in your room that night. But then you decide to invite all your friends to spend the night. In this case, your room is going to be really

Materials
* small pot
* knife
* 6 lemons, limes, or oranges
* small glass or plastic jar with lid
* wooden spoon
* an adult
* stove

crowded. No doubt you will have trouble getting permission to invite all these friends. But perhaps you can get away with it if you point out that you and your friends are examining the difference between dilute and concentrated solutions.

Having only two people in your room is like a dilute solution. Only a few solutes may be present in the solvent. Having all your friends in your room is like a concentrated solution. In this case, the same amount of solvent will contain many more solutes. You can easily turn a concentrated solution into a dilute one. You do this whenever you make a glass of orange juice by adding water to a concentrate. But how can you make a concentrated solution from a dilute one? It is just as easy.

Under adult supervision, cut 6 lemons, limes, or oranges into small pieces and squeeze the juice into a small pot. Be sure to remove the pits. Heat the juice gently while stirring and continue heating until the juice begins to thicken. Allow the concentrated juice to cool. You can bottle and refrigerate the lime or lemon juice to use as a flavoring or freeze the orange juice and dilute it for breakfast one morning. While everyone is enjoying the juice, be sure to share what you have learned about solutes, solvents, and dilute and concentrated solutions.

Heating causes the water in the fruit juice to evaporate, leaving behind all the solutes. Because there are many more solutes but much less solvent, the solution is now concentrated. If you continue heating the juice until all the water evaporates, all that will be left are the solutes. These are mostly the sugars, vitamins, and minerals that are present in juice. The only other thing that will be left is a messy pot to clean!

Experiment 1.4

How Can You Keep Fruits and Salads Fresh?

Fruit juices are solutions that contain various solutes dissolved in water. For example, orange juice contains several solutes, including sugars, minerals, and vitamins, especially vitamin C. Vitamin C has a chemical name—ascorbic acid. Without vitamin C, your body could not stay intact. The soft tissues

Materials
✳ large drinking glass
✳ an adult
✳ knife
✳ orange juice
✳ apple
✳ 2 plates
✳ water

in your joints and gums would start to fall apart, causing bleeding. Injured tissue would not be able to repair itself.

Because your body cannot make vitamin C, you must get it from foods and beverages. Which products shown in Figure 5 contain vitamin C? Many people also take vitamin C tablets. Besides being required for good health, vitamin C can also be used to keep foods fresh. In other words, vitamin C can be used as a preservative. Here is your chance to see what you can keep fresh with vitamin C.

Under adult supervision cut an apple into mouth-sized slices. Soak half the slices in orange juice. After soaking them for 30 minutes, remove the apple slices and rinse them with water. Set up two groups. Place those soaked in orange juice on one plate. Place those that were not soaked in orange juice in a second group. Compare what happens to the apples on each plate. Which ones turn brown sooner? You should now realize

lemon   tangerine   lime

grapefruit   potatoes

Figure 5. All these supermarket items contain vitamin C. However, the citrus fruits shown here are rich in vitamin C compared with the potatoes.

why chefs sometimes squeeze a lemon or lime over a Waldorf salad, which contains freshly cut apples.

By the way, here is your chance to really "play" with your food and friends at the same time! Invite your friends to your home and ask each one to bring a different brand of juice or a different piece of fruit. Experiment to see which type of juice—orange, lemon, lime, grapefruit, cranberry, grape, or pineapple—works best as a preservative. Which type of fruit— pear, banana, peach, or kiwi—is preserved the best? Which combination of fruit juice and fruit works best?

Experiment 1.5

How Much Vitamin C Does Orange Juice Contain?

As you might guess, fruit juices have a higher vitamin C content than other beverages such as sodas and milk. But exactly how much vitamin C does a glass of orange juice contain? The best way to find out is to analyze it for its vitamin C content. Several procedures are available to determine the vitamin C content of a solution. One such procedure is straightforward, as you can see in this experiment.

Place a 500 mg vitamin C tablet inside a paper towel and crush it by pressing down with a spoon. Dissolve the crushed vitamin C in 500 mL of water. You now have a vitamin C solution with a concentration of 500 mg/500 mL, or 1 mg/mL. Spray the inside of a clean glass jar with spray starch. Pour 50 mL of the vitamin C solution into the jar. How many mg of vitamin C have you added to the jar? Gently swirl the jar so that the spray starch and vitamin C solution mix.

Use a dropper to add Lugol's iodine to the vitamin C/ starch solution. Almost every biology classroom has Lugol's iodine for staining specimens to view under a microscope. Ask a biology teacher for a small bottle. Explain that you need it for an experiment you are doing on vitamin C. Be careful not to spill the Lugol's iodine, because it will stain your hands and clothes.

Notice that the vitamin C/starch solution turns blue-black when a drop of Lugol's iodine is added. Gently swirl the jar. The blue-black color will disappear. When the iodine is added, it first reacts with the starch to form a blue-black color. Swirling the jar causes the iodine to react with the vitamin C. When this happens, the blue-black color disappears. Keeping count of the number of drops you add, continue adding the Lugol's iodine drop by drop until the blue-black color no longer disappears. At this point, the iodine has reacted with all the vitamin C that is present. The iodine can now react with the starch where it remains to form the blue-black color. How many drops must you add to the vitamin C/starch solution to reach the point where the blue-black color remains?

Repeat the procedure, this time using 50 mL of an orange juice solution rather than the vitamin C solution. Be sure to first clean the jar and then spray it with spray starch. Add the orange juice. Count the number of drops of Lugol's iodine needed to allow the blue-black color to remain in the juice solution. How does this number compare with what you added to the vitamin C solution? The more drops of Lugol's iodine you add, the more vitamin C is present in the sample. If you added more drops to the orange juice, then it contained more than 50 mg of vitamin C. You can calculate the actual amount of vitamin C in the orange juice by using the following equation.

$$\frac{\text{drops iodine added to vitamin C solution}}{50 \text{ mg vitamin C}} = \frac{\text{drops iodine added to orange juice}}{x \text{ mg vitamin C}}$$

Just plug in the number of drops of Lugol's iodine you added in each case. Then solve for *x* to calculate how many mg of vitamin C are in 50 mL of the orange juice you tested.

Project Idea

Testing Beverages for Vitamin C Content

You can test a wide variety of solutions, including juices made from concentrates and freshly squeezed fruit. What happens if you bring the solution to a boil and then test it for vitamin C? You can also determine how stable vitamin C is. Test a solution left in the refrigerator every day to determine how much vitamin C is present. What happens to the vitamin C content if the solution is not refrigerated but left on the kitchen counter for several days?

Expand your project to test other beverages for their vitamin C content. You can analyze orange-flavored sodas, fruit punches, and any product that advertises it has a high vitamin C content. Calculate how much of each product you would have to drink to obtain the recommended daily requirement of vitamin C. Prepare a table summarizing your findings.

Experiment 1.6

How Can You Get Rid of a Solute?

All sodas basically contain the same solutes dissolved in water. These include a sweet syrup, artificial flavorings, and a gas to give the soda a bubbly taste. The gas is a chemical known as carbon dioxide, the same gas you give off when you breathe

Materials

* unopened 2-liter bottle of soda

* small balloon (the smaller the better)

out. Sodas can give off their carbon dioxide, too. When a soda loses its carbon dioxide, it tastes flat. In this experiment, you will use the carbon dioxide gas a soda gives off to inflate a balloon. By the way, this is an experiment you can keep an eye on while you do your homework.

Unscrew the cap from an unopened 2-liter bottle of soda. Quickly place the balloon over the mouth of the bottle and set it aside. Start doing your homework. As you do your homework, watch the balloon inflate as the carbon dioxide gas escapes from the soda. If you do not have much homework, you may finish before the balloon has inflated. In that case, experiment with ways of trying to get the carbon dioxide out of the soda faster. Think about what happens to sodas on a hot day at the beach. Also, do you remember the time you opened a soda after it rattled around in the trunk of a car?

Experiment 1.7

How Does Temperature Affect Dissolving?

Materials

* small pot
* measuring cup
* stove
* an adult
* water
* teaspoon
* Celsius thermometer (ask your science teacher for one)
* sugar
* instant coffee or tea bag (optional)

Some people drink their coffee black. Some people drink their tea straight. In other words, these people do not add any other solutes to the water other than the coffee or tea. But most people add at least one solute— sugar. You may not enjoy the taste of either coffee or tea, but you may enjoy experimenting with them.

Temperature affects how much solute can dissolve in a solvent. In some cases, raising the temperature allows more solute to dissolve in the same amount of solvent. In other cases, the opposite is observed. Raising the temperature causes less solute to be dissolved in the solvent. Where does sugar fit in?

Pour one cup of water into a pot. **Under adult supervision,** heat the water until the temperature reaches and stays at 30°C. While stirring, add one teaspoon of sugar at a time. Determine how many teaspoons of sugar will dissolve in one cup of water at 30°C. When you are finished, you can add some instant coffee or drop a tea bag into the water. Just make sure that whoever drinks the coffee or tea likes it with a lot of sugar! If they do not like it so sweet, how can they dilute the solution?

Repeat the procedure, using water temperatures of 40°C, 50°C, and 60°C. In each case, count the number of teaspoons of sugar that dissolve in the cup of water.

Prepare a table and a graph of your data as shown in Figure 6. How does temperature affect the dissolving of sugar in water? Which would need more sugar to have the same degree of sweetness—hot tea or iced tea?

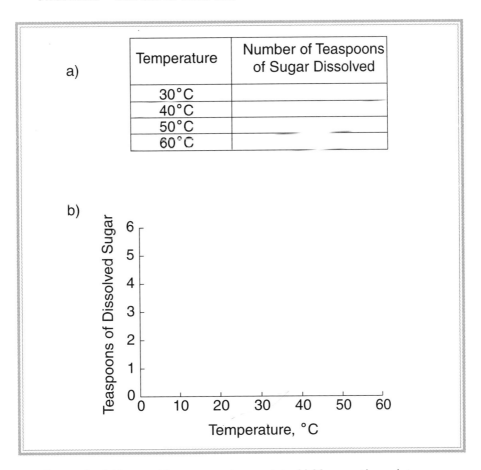

Figure 6. a) Use a table to record your data. b) You can then plot your data to determine whether there is any connection between the two variables you are working with in an experiment. Notice that the independent variable, the temperature, is always plotted on the x-axis. The dependent variable is plotted on the y-axis.

Chapter 2

Dairy Products

You learned in Chapter 1 that solutes dissolve in a solvent to produce a solution. In a solution, the solutes become so small that you can see them only with a very powerful microscope. Because the solutes are so small, the solution becomes clear and transparent. But not all substances will dissolve in a solvent to produce a solution. In some cases, a substance does not completely dissolve to become invisible. Instead, the substance forms particles that are larger than those found in solutions. Although they are quite small, these particles remain large enough to be evenly suspended or spread throughout the liquid. Whenever two substances are mixed so that one becomes suspended, but not dissolved, in the other, a **colloid** has been prepared. A colloid contains small particles that remain suspended in a substance, which is usually a liquid.

Examples of colloids you can find at a supermarket include butter, whipped cream, gelatin desserts, mustard, jelly, and ketchup. In each of these, substances are broken down into particles that are suspended in a liquid. For example, butter consists of water particles that are suspended in liquid fats. Whipped cream is made by suspending the gas particles present in air in heavy cream. Ketchup is prepared by crushing tomatoes, sugar, and spices and then suspending them in water and vinegar.

The particles suspended in a colloid can be brought closer together. If enough particles are clumped together, either the colloid will turn into a solid or a solid mass of material will form within the colloid. Whenever you prepare a gelatin dessert, you begin by suspending the powdered materials in water to form a colloid. Refrigerating the colloid causes the particles to come together, turning the colloid into a solid that can be eaten. How would you change the solid back into a colloid?

Experiment 2.1

How Can You Turn Milk into Cheese?

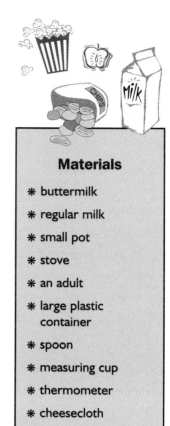

In addition to changing the temperature, another way to clump the particles in a colloid is to add certain chemicals. You can check this out in an experiment using milk, which is another example of a colloid. One of the solutes in milk is a sugar called lactose. Some people cannot digest or break down the lactose. As a result the lactose remains in their digestive tract where it can cause cramps, bloating, and diarrhea. To avoid these problems, people with this condition must drink lactose-free milk. Unlike regular milk, lactose-free milk will never turn sour. Given enough time, the lactose in regular milk turns into another chemical called lactic acid, which has a sour taste.

Materials

* buttermilk
* regular milk
* small pot
* stove
* an adult
* large plastic container
* spoon
* measuring cup
* thermometer
* cheesecloth
* rennin tablet

You can always tell if milk is sour by tasting it. But you really do not want to do that. Fortunately there is a more pleasant way. Just look for clumps in the milk. These clumps are all the particles, including lactic acid, that come together when milk sours. Both cheese and cream cheese are made by first clumping all the particles in milk. Here is how to make your own cheese.

Add about 1 fluid ounce of buttermilk to about 200 fluid

ounces of regular milk in a plastic container. Stir to mix the buttermilk and the milk. The buttermilk contains a chemical that will cause the lactose to turn into lactic acid rather quickly. But it does take some time, so allow the container to stand for at least four hours. While you are waiting, you can use the leftover buttermilk to make pancakes.

Pour the milk sample into a pot. **Under adult supervision,** gently warm the milk to around 30°C. While stirring, add a crushed rennin tablet to the milk. Rennin is sold in supermarkets under the trade name Junket. Slowly increase the temperature of the milk to 38°C. Do not allow the temperature to get above 38°C. Continue stirring and heating for several minutes.

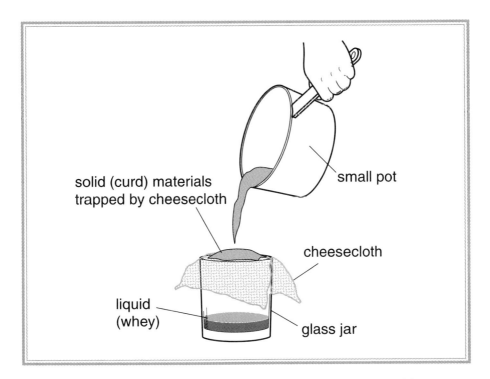

solid (curd) materials
trapped by cheesecloth

small pot

cheesecloth

liquid
(whey)

glass jar

Figure 7. Cheesecloth is very useful for separating solid material from a liquid. Just be sure to pour the mixture through the cheesecloth slowly.

Examine the contents of your pot. If you wish, you can collect the clumped particles (your cheese!) by filtering the contents of the pot through cheesecloth, as shown in Figure 7. Can you guess how cheesecloth got its name? Allow the solids to dry. The solids are known as the *curd*, and the liquid that passed through the cheesecloth is called the *whey*. Add some salt and taste your cheese. Unfortunately, it will not taste anything like the cheese you find at the supermarket. Commercial cheese is prepared in a more elaborate manner and is slowly aged to give it flavor and texture. Do not try aging yours because it will probably spoil. Cheese makers add chemicals to prevent spoiling.

Project Idea

Turning Milk into Glue

Adding vinegar to milk and then heating it produces a gluelike substance. Pour 125 mL of nonfat milk and 25 mL of vinegar into a small pot. **Under adult supervision**, heat the mixture gently while stirring continuously until small lumps begin to form. Remove the pot from the stove and continue to stir until no more lumps form. Allow the lumps to settle and then filter the mixture through cheesecloth to collect the curds. Return the solid to the pot. Add 30 mL of water to the solid and stir. Add 1/2 teaspoon of baking soda. Observe what happens. Continue to add a little more baking soda until no more bubbles appear. Scrape out the solid material from the pot and test its adhesive properties.

Try to develop the most adhesive glue by varying the proportions of the ingredients. Compare the properties of your product with commercial glues. You can test their adhesive properties on paper, wood, and metal objects. If your product glues two things together, how long does it work compared with commercial products? Check the Internet to learn more about the chemistry of glue making.

Experiment 2.2

What Is the Mineral Content of Milk?

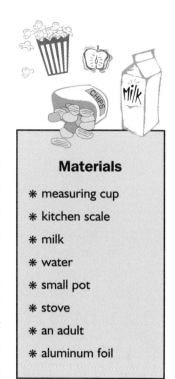

Rather than clump all the solutes in milk at once, you can also isolate each type of solute and determine how much of it is present. For example, you can determine the mineral and protein content of milk. The minerals include calcium, magnesium, zinc, phosphorus, and iron, all of which are needed for good health. These minerals are dissolved in milk. The proteins are much larger and, therefore, are

Materials

* measuring cup
* kitchen scale
* milk
* water
* small pot
* stove
* an adult
* aluminum foil

suspended, rather than dissolved, in the milk. Like the minerals, the proteins can be easily separated from everything else that is in milk.

Weigh a measuring cup on a kitchen scale. Pour some milk into the measuring cup and weigh it again. Calculate the mass of the milk by subtracting the mass of the measuring cup from the mass of the measuring cup and milk. Pour some water into a pot. Cover the pot with aluminum foil, making a depression in the middle. Punch small holes through the foil near the inside rim of the pot, as shown in Figure 8. Remove the foil, weigh it, and then replace it on the pot. Carefully pour the milk into the depression.

Under adult supervision, gently heat the milk on a stove to evaporate the water (the solvent) in milk. Continue heating

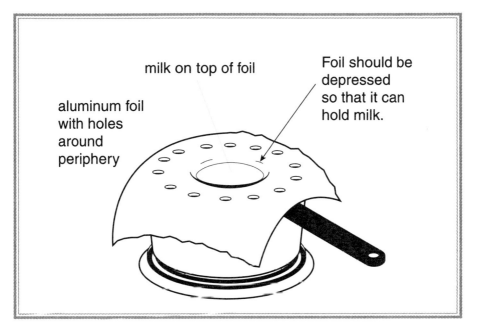

milk on top of foil

Foil should be depressed so that it can hold milk.

aluminum foil with holes around periphery

Figure 8. Heat from the stove will evaporate most of the solvent in milk, leaving the minerals in the aluminum foil. Why should you punch small holes in the aluminum foil before heating the water in the pot?

until all that remains on the aluminum foil are brownish-black ashes. Be sure that there is always enough water in the pot. If you must add more water, turn off the heat and wait until the pot has cooled. Then carefully lift the foil and pour more water into the pot. Continue heating until only ashes remain. Allow everything to cool and remove the foil, making sure not to lose any ashes. Weigh the foil and ashes.

The ashes represent the minerals that have remained after evaporating the water and other combustible substances in milk. A combustible substance is one that will burn. Calculate the mineral content of the milk by placing your data in the following equation.

$$\frac{\text{mass of ash}}{\text{mass of milk}} \times 100 = \text{percent mineral content}$$

This experiment brings up another issue. Mass and weight are not the same. Mass is a constant, whereas weight can vary. For example, your mass is the "stuff" that makes up your body. No matter where you are, your mass does not change. Your weight, however, can change, depending on where you are. Weight is the attraction that gravity exerts on mass. On the moon where gravity exerts less force, you would weigh less but still have the same mass.

Experiment 2.3

What Is the Protein Content of Milk?

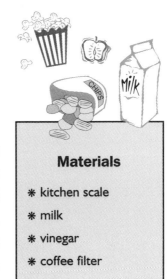

Here is your chance to design your own procedure. Keep in mind what you did to determine the mineral content of milk in Experiment 2.2. If you add vinegar slowly to milk while stirring, the proteins will form solid clumps. There is no need to

Materials

* kitchen scale
* milk
* vinegar
* coffee filter

heat the mixture. You can separate the protein clumps from the rest of the milk by using a coffee filter. Be sure to weigh whatever needs to be weighed so that you know how much milk and proteins you have. Then use the equation given in

---

Project Idea

Comparing Milk Brands

Test as many different milk brands as possible for mineral and protein content. Because you need only a small amount, you can ask friends and neighbors for some milk. Be sure to test reduced fat and nonfat milks. Compare your results with the information listed on the labels on the milk containers. Use the Internet to contact the American Dairy Association <http://www.adsa.uiuc.edu> for information to include in your project. Check the library for information on what role the various minerals play in good health.

Experiment 2.2, this time substituting the mass of protein for the mass of ash to determine the protein content in milk.

Butter versus Margarine

In recent years, people have switched from butter to margarine to reduce the level of cholesterol in their blood. Studies have shown that a high level of cholesterol can interfere with blood flow through the body by causing the arteries to harden. This interruption of blood flow increases the risk of a heart attack. Butter is made from animal fats. Margarine is a fat that is made from vegetable oils. To understand the difference between an animal fat and a vegetable oil, you need to take a brief look at some chemistry.

Both fats and oils are organic compounds. You may be familiar with the word *organic* from having heard the phrases "organically grown" or "contains only natural, organic ingredients." An **organic compound** is defined as any chemical substance that contains the element carbon. You can think of an **element** as the building block of a chemical compound. There are some exceptions to this definition of an organic compound, but there is no need to be concerned about those exceptions here. In addition to carbon, fats and oils also contain the elements oxygen and hydrogen.

Butter and Margarine Are Lipids

Fats and oils are classified as lipids. A fat is a solid lipid at room temperature, whereas an oil is a liquid lipid at room temperature. A **lipid** is an organic compound that is characterized by having many more carbon and hydrogen atoms than oxygen atoms. For example, examine the following chemical formula for a lipid: $C_{57}H_{110}O_6$. A **chemical formula** is a shorthand method for providing some information about a chemical compound. The formula for the fat tells you that there are 57 carbon atoms, 110 hydrogen atoms, and only 6 oxygen atoms in this compound. Recall from the Introduction that an atom is the smallest unit of a chemical substance such as an element.

A chemical formula does not provide enough information to show the important difference between animal fats and vegetable oils. In order to understand this difference, you must examine another type of formula called a **structural formula**. A structural formula shows the arrangement of all the atoms of

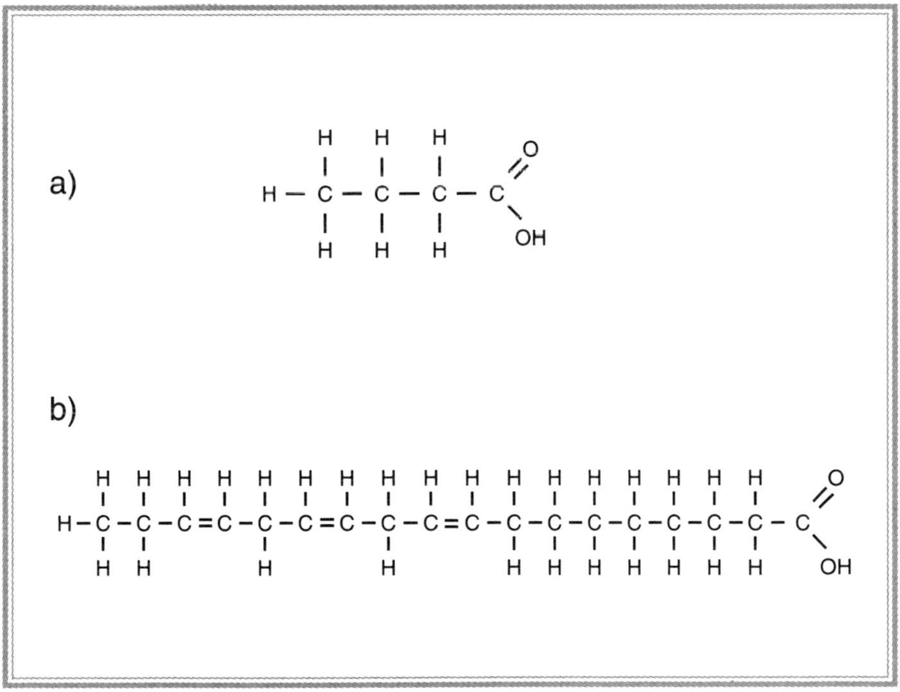

Figure 9. Both these compounds are known as fatty acids. Notice that both these compounds have a –COOH group of atoms at the end. Locate this group. This group makes these compounds fatty acids.

the various elements in a compound. For example, Figure 9a shows the structural formula for a compound found in butter. Compare this structural formula to the one shown in Figure 9b, which shows a compound found in vegetable oil. What similarities do you notice? What differences do you see?

If you examine the lines connecting several of the carbon atoms in the vegetable oil, you will see that double lines are present in three places. No double lines are present between the carbon atoms in the animal oil. These lines, whether single or double, represent chemical bonds. A **chemical bond** joins one atom to another. Whenever a fat contains one or more double bonds that connect carbon atoms, it is said to be **unsaturated**. What is a polyunsaturated fat? If all these bonds are single ones, the fat is said to be **saturated**. Animal fats are avoided because their saturated fats raise cholesterol levels.

Qualitative Observations versus Quantitative Observations

You can easily determine if a food contains either unsaturated or saturated fats. Just think how greasy your hands feel after eating French fries at a fast-food restaurant. The French fries are coated with fats from being cooked in hot oil. To test a food sample for fat, just rub some of it on a brown paper bag. Look for any grease stains that appear. In this case, you are making a qualitative observation. A **qualitative observation** involves simply noting whether some characteristic is present or absent. By looking for a grease stain, you are simply determining whether a food sample contains or does not contain fat. But scientists often make quantitative observations. A **quantitative observation** involves determining numerical information, for example, how much fat the food sample contains. Your experiments in determining the mineral and protein content of milk involved quantitative observations. Experiment 2.4 involves making quantitative observations about fat.

Experiment 2.4

Can You Measure How Unsaturated a Fat Is?

Materials

* several different vegetable oils
* science teacher to supervise
* iodine crystals
* safety goggles
* hexane
* science lab ventilating hood
* balance accurate to 0.01 g
* dropper
* graduated cylinder or pipettes
* test tubes
* beaker

Unsaturated fats will react with iodine. As Figure 10 shows, a double bond can be broken, making room for iodine atoms. The more double bonds present, the more that can be broken, and the more iodine that can be added until all the double bonds have been changed into single ones. At that point, any additional iodine that is added to the saturated compound would not react with the oil but remain in solution. Thus the solution turns violet at this point. Iodine cannot be added to a saturated fat because there are no double bonds that can be broken. Thus, just a drop or two of iodine to a saturated fat will cause the solution to turn violet.

You can test various vegetable oils to see which is the most unsaturated. You must work with a physical science or chemistry teacher because of the equipment and materials needed for this experiment. You will need a balance accurate enough to weigh 0.05 g of iodine crystals. You will also need a solvent that will dissolve iodine crystals. Water is not a good choice in this case. Because fats and water do not mix, you

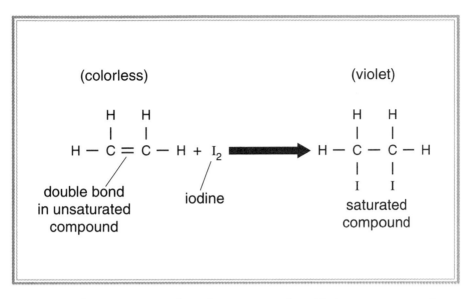

Figure 10. Notice where the iodine atoms can be added to an unsaturated fat. Once all the double bonds are broken, then the compound is said to be "saturated" because it cannot hold any more atoms.

must use a solvent that will dissolve the iodine crystals and then be able to mix with the oils. Such a solvent must be a nonpolar, organic solvent.

You know what organic means, but what is the difference between nonpolar and polar? Simply stated, a **polar compound** has regions with different electric charges. In the case of water, one end of the compound has a negative charge, while the other end has a positive charge. A **nonpolar compound** does not have regions with different electric charges. Instead, different regions of the compound have the same charge, or the charge is evenly distributed. Oils are nonpolar compounds and can be dissolved only with nonpolar solvents. A phrase that is used in chemistry is "like dissolves like." Now you should understand what this statement means.

Care must be used when selecting a nonpolar, organic

solvent to dissolve fats. Perhaps the safest nonpolar, organic compound to use is hexane. Be sure to use a ventilating hood under your teacher's supervision when using hexane. Also be sure to wear safety goggles. Dissolve 0.05 g of iodine crystals in a beaker of 100 mL of hexane. In a test tube, mix 5 mL of hexane with 5 mL of the oil being tested, and then add the iodine solution a drop at a time. You can test various vegetable oils, including olive, peanut, sunflower, walnut, corn, coconut, and canola oils. Count the number of drops of iodine needed to turn the oil-hexane mixture violet.

Set up a table showing your results in degrees of unsaturation. Your table will be based on the oil that requires the fewest drops before turning violet. Use this oil as the basis for calculating the degree of unsaturation of the other oils. For example, if another oil takes twice as many iodine drops, then this oil is twice as unsaturated.

Making Margarine and Butter

If margarine contains vegetable oil, then how can it be a solid? The answer can be found in the process that is used to make margarine. Margarine is made using a procedure similar to the one you used in Experiment 2.4 when you added iodine to break the double bonds in the unsaturated fats in oil. In the case of margarine, the procedure is called hydrogenation. This means that a double bond between two carbon atoms in the unsaturated fat is broken and two hydrogen atoms are added, as shown in Figure 11.

The double bonds make the unsaturated fat a liquid (oil) at room temperature. By adding hydrogen, some of the double bonds are changed to single bonds. When a certain number of

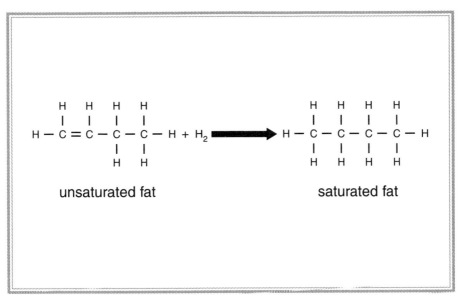

Figure 11. An unsaturated fat can be turned into a saturated fat by breaking the double bond and adding hydrogen atoms.

double bonds have been changed into single bonds, the liquid oil becomes a solid. In other words, margarine is nothing more than a hydrogenated vegetable oil. Tell someone that the next time they spread margarine on toast or put it on a baked potato.

You may find a hydrogenated vegetable oil not only in your refrigerator but also in a kitchen cabinet. Hydrogenated vegetable oil is the main ingredient in a product known as solid shortening. Mix two tablespoons of water with one cup of shortening and you have margarine. It will not taste like the real thing because the margarine in your refrigerator contains salt, artificial color, and artificial flavors to improve its taste and appearance. In fact, the margarine you make from shortening may taste more like the margarine that first appeared in supermarkets. Concerned about the possible loss of business when margarine first appeared, butter manufacturers pressured politicians into passing laws that required margarine to be both unappetizing and unappealing. The margarine first sold in supermarkets did not taste great and had a very unpleasant brown color.

Project Idea

The Perfect Diet

Many people are concerned about their diets. Some people avoid eating fats at all costs. Yet everyone needs some fat as a part of his or her regular diet to stay healthy. Search the library and the Internet for information on diets. How do they compare in terms of their fat recommendations and total calorie intake? Look especially for information concerning any long-term studies. For example, which diets, if any, claim to be successful in maintaining a weight loss two or three years after a person started their program? Also check for information about substances known as trans fatty acids, which are present in margarine. How do they affect diet recommendations? Summarize all your findings in a written report.

Experiment 2.5

How Did Your Great-Grandmother Make Butter?

All you need to make butter is some heavy cream and a large, plastic container. Half fill the container with heavy cream. Cover it tightly and shake vigorously. It may help if you do this while listening to your favorite rock group. Keep checking the cream every five minutes to see whether you have made butter. Although this is a simple, but exhausting, way to make butter, this is not the way your great-grandmother made it. Besides, she probably would not have liked the music.

Refrigerate about 2 cups raw milk for several hours in a large glass jar to allow the cream to collect at the top. The colder the milk, the thicker the cream. Check with your local supermarket or farm to see whether they can get some raw milk for you.

Use a large spoon with holes to skim the cream from the milk. If you do not have at least a half cup of cream, refrigerate some more raw milk to get more cream. The milk should run through the holes, but the cream should remain

Materials

* 2 cups raw (nonhomogenized) milk
* large glass jar
* heavy cream
* large spoon with small holes that will fit into the glass jar
* refrigerator
* plastic container and cover
* butter churn or a plastic spatula and mixing bowl
* flat wooden spoon
* bowl
* cold water
* salt

in the spoon. If the spoon does not have holes, try to pour off any milk that collects in the spoon. Allow the cream to sit at room temperature for 24 hours so that it begins to sour. The butter will not separate easily from cream if it has not turned sour.

Put the cream in a butter churn if you are fortunate enough to have one. Otherwise, a small plastic spatula and a large mixing bowl can be used, but be aware that your arm will probably get tired. Churn the butter in a steady and methodical motion, turning the paddle or spatula about one revolution every second. Separating the butter from the cream is not a fast process. You may have to churn anywhere from thirty minutes to several hours, depending on the quality of the cream. When one arm gets tired, switch to the other one. You know you are on the right track when the cream begins to thicken. Examine the top of the cream periodically to look for the butter that will form at the surface. What is underneath is now called buttermilk.

Carefully remove the butter from the top of the buttermilk with a flat wooden spoon. Place the butter in a bowl. Use the spoon to work the butter back and forth on the sides of the bowl. Pour off any buttermilk that comes to the surface. Pour a small amount of very cold water into the bowl and work the butter as you did before. When the water becomes discolored, pour it out. Add some more cold water and repeat the process until the water remains clear. You want to get all the buttermilk out of the butter or else it will spoil. Sprinkle a pinch of salt and mix it in. Keep your butter refrigerated.

Experiment 2.6

How Can You Mix Oil and Vinegar?

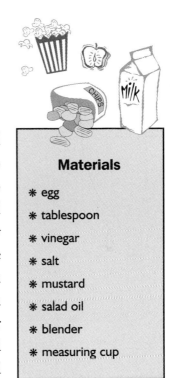

Materials

* egg
* tablespoon
* vinegar
* salt
* mustard
* salad oil
* blender
* measuring cup

Have you ever tried to mix oil and vinegar to make a salad dressing? No matter how hard you shake the two liquids, once you stop, the oil collects as tiny drops that eventually come together and separate from the vinegar. Obviously oil does not form either a solution or colloid with vinegar. However, if another substance is added, then the oil and vinegar will not separate. Instead they will remain mixed so that one liquid remains distributed as small drops in the other liquid. Whenever two liquids are prepared in this way, an emulsion has been made. The substance that is added to make the **emulsion** is called an **emulsifier**. Figure 12 shows how an emulsifier acts as a bridge between two liquids that normally do not mix. Eggs are good emulsifiers. You can see for yourself by using an egg to make mayonnaise.

Mix one egg, one tablespoon of vinegar, ½ teaspoon of salt, ½ teaspoon of mustard, and ¼ cup of salad oil in a blender. Blend this mixture for several seconds. Add ¾ cup of salad oil to the mixture in a slow, steady stream while blending, until most of the oil is absorbed to form an emulsion. This is your mayonnaise.

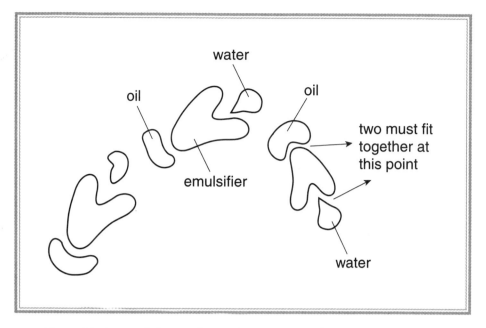

Figure 12. An emulsifier can be used to mix two substances that normally do not mix. One end of an emulsifier attracts one substance, such as water. The other end of the emulsifier attracts the other substance, such as oil, bringing the two substances together.

Experiment with ways of making mayonnaise by varying the proportions or testing different ingredients. For example, substitute lemon juice in place of vinegar. Check a cookbook on how to use an emulsifier to make Hollandaise sauce. Who knows—this may be the start of your career as one of the great chefs of the world, if not your neighborhood.

Chapter 3

Fruits and Vegetables

The most colorful aisle in a supermarket is the fruit and vegetable section. Just picture all the colors that you can find there—the reds in apples and tomatoes, the yellows in lemons and grapefruits, the purples in plums and eggplants, the greens in lettuce and limes, and the oranges in carrots and, of course, oranges. All these colors are due to chemicals known as pigments that are present in these fruits and vegetables. A **pigment** is a chemical substance that has a characteristic color. Dyes are pigments that are used to color materials and substances, including a variety of foods to make them more appealing to consumers.

Experiment 3.1

Have You Ever Used Fruits or Vegetables to Decorate a Cake?

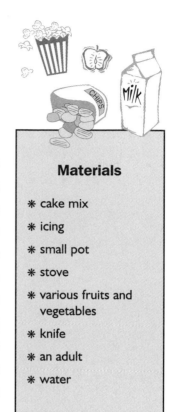

Many dyes are obtained from chemicals in coal, which are then turned into compounds that can be added to foods. However, studies have shown that some of these chemicals can cause cancer in laboratory animals. As a result, the United States Food and Drug Administration has banned the use of certain dyes, such as red dye number 2, in food. Rather than depend on coal for dyes, however, you can use fruits and vegetables.

Materials

* cake mix
* icing
* small pot
* stove
* various fruits and vegetables
* knife
* an adult
* water

Under adult supervision, bake a cake, following the directions on the box. Next make a white icing or use a prepared one. To extract the dye from fruits and vegetables, first cut one into small pieces and then boil it in water. Not all the dyes dissolve equally well in water, so you will have to experiment to see which ones are best to use. First test a small sample of each fruit and vegetable before you try to extract a dye to use. Start with oranges, lemons, and red cabbage. Continue heating the water until it has a distinct color. Allow the dye solution to cool. Add several drops of the dye solution to your icing. Try mixing different dyes to see what colors you can obtain. How many different colors does your cake have?

Invite your friends to share the cake and be sure to tell them that no artificial colors have been added to the icing.

Acids and Bases

You might remember as a child that swallowing aspirin was not a pleasant experience. Even if children's aspirin is sweetened and mixed with something like applesauce, it still tastes sour. The sour taste is due to the active ingredient in aspirin. This active ingredient is an organic compound called acetylsalicylic acid. You read in Chapter 2 that an organic compound is one that contains the element carbon, usually in combination with the elements hydrogen, oxygen, and nitrogen. Figure 13 shows why acetylsalicylic acid is classified as an organic compound.

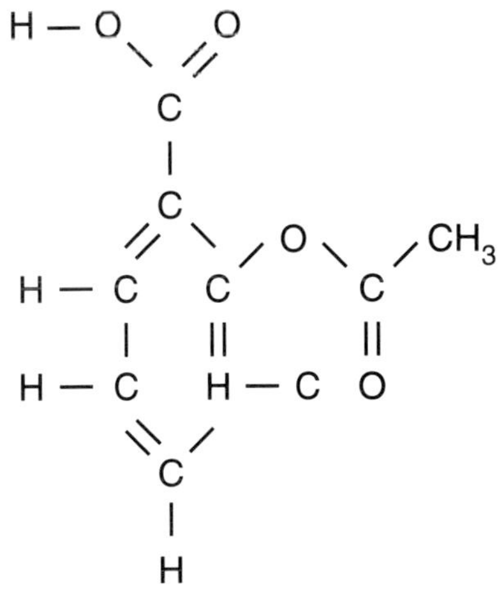

Figure 13. Aspirin is an organic compound because it contains the element carbon. What other elements are present in aspirin?

Acetylsalicylic acid is the third acid you have encountered so far in this book. In Experiment 1.4 and Experiment 1.5, a chemical called ascorbic acid (vitamin C) was mentioned. In Experiment 2.1, you learned that milk turns sour when lactic acid is formed. What exactly do all these chemicals have in common in order to be classified as acids? All acids have distinctive properties, including a sour taste. You probably realize how sour a lemon tastes. Its sour taste is due to the citric acid it contains. An acid is a chemical substance that can be defined in several different ways. A general definition of an **acid** is a chemical substance whose water solution has a sour taste and that reacts with metals to produce a gas.

As a child, you may have also gotten soap in your mouth while washing your face. If you did, then you know how bitter soap tastes. You may have dropped a bar of soap when showering. That is easy to do because soap is very slippery. The bitter taste and slippery feeling of soap are two properties of another group of compounds known as bases. Soap is a base. A **base** is a chemical with certain distinctive properties, such as a bitter taste and slippery feeling. But you really do not want to taste something to tell whether it is an acid because of its sour taste, or a base because of its bitter taste. Tasting a chemical is not a good idea unless you know that it is some type of food.

Experiment 3.2

Is It an Acid or a Base?

How can you tell if something is an acid or a base without tasting it? This experiment will show you how the dye from red cabbage can be used to tell whether something is an acid or a base. The purplish pigment in red cabbage is an indicator. An **indicator** is a pigment that changes color, depending on whether it is added to a solution that is an acid or a base.

Under adult supervision, chop the leaves from a red cabbage into small pieces. Place the pieces in a blender and cover them with water.

Materials

* red cabbage
* knife
* an adult
* blender, or a small pot and stove
* water
* plastic or glass container
* small glasses
* measuring cup
* white vinegar
* household ammonia
* masking tape and marker

Cover and blend until the contents have become liquefied. If a blender is not available, or if you do not feel like cleaning the mess, place the small pieces of red cabbage in a small pot. Cover the cabbage with water and slowly boil the contents until the water turns a dark color. You may have to add some water to prevent the cabbage from burning.

After allowing the pot to cool, carefully pour the liquid into a clean, dry container. Mix 10 mL of cabbage juice with 10 mL of white vinegar in a small glass. Vinegar is an acid. What color does the red cabbage dye turn when it is mixed with an acid? Label this jar. Next mix 10 mL of the cabbage juice and household ammonia. The ammonia is a base. What color does the red dye turn when it is mixed with a base? Label this jar. Now test every solution that you can find in your house! Compare the color of different solutions to your two known jars of acid and base. Make a table listing each solution either as an acid or a base depending on the color it turned when you added the dye.

Acid Precipitation

The degree to which a solution is acidic can be expressed numerically as pH. The **pH** is a quantitative expression of the acidity of a solution. The pH scale ranges from 0 to 14, with 7 being neutral. Any solution with a pH value less than 7 is acidic. The lower the pH, the more acidic the solution. Any solution with a pH value higher than 7 is said to be basic. The higher the pH, the more basic the solution. Like an acid, a base can be defined in several different ways. Now that you know what pH represents, you can define both acid and base quantitatively rather than qualitatively. *A solution with a pH value less than 7 is acidic, and a solution with a pH value greater than 7 is basic.* Figure 14 shows the pH of some common household items.

Normally, the pH of rain and snow is 5.5. Thus, both are slightly acidic. In fact, all forms of precipitation—rain, snow, sleet, and hail—are acidic. That is why the term *acid precipitation* is used. Acid precipitation is caused by burning fossil fuels such as coal and oil. When these fuels are burned, gases are released and rise into the atmosphere. Here these gases react with the water in the atmosphere to produce acids. These acids fall back to Earth when it rains or snows. As a

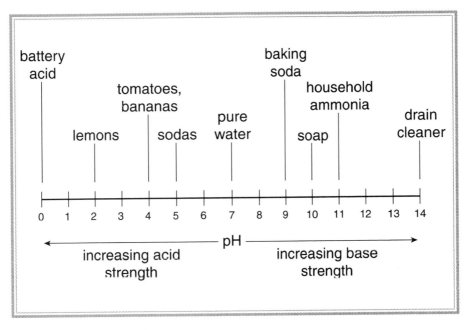

Figure 14. Which of the household items is the most acidic? Which is the most basic?

result, the acidity of rain and snow increases, often having a pH value of 3.

The most acidic rainfall in the United States occurred in Wheeling, West Virginia, where the pH was measured at 1.5. A drop in pH from 5.5 to 1.5 may not seem that significant to you. But each unit on the pH scale represents a tenfold change in concentration. Thus, rainfall with a pH value of 1.5 is 10,000 times more acidic than a rainfall with a pH value of 5.5.

Experiment 3.3

What Is the pH of Rain?

Acid precipitation is becoming a major environmental problem in many parts of the country as more gases are released into the atmosphere. Is acid precipitation a problem in your community? This experiment will examine the pH of the precipitation in your community and show how acid precipitation can affect certain structures, such as marble statues.

Materials
* red cabbage juice
* measuring cup
* rain or snow
* small glass jars
* lemon juice
* seashells
* vinegar
* pH paper

Extract the pigment from red cabbage as described in Experiment 3.2. Use the pigment solution to test the pH of the rain or any other form of precipitation in your local area. Pour 5 mL of the red cabbage solution into a clean glass jar. Collect some rain or snow and add a measured amount to the red cabbage solution. What color does the solution turn? Mix 5 mL of the red cabbage solution with lemon juice. Add a volume of lemon juice equal to the volume of rain or snow you added. The pH of lemon juice is 2. Compare the color of the pigment/precipitation mixture with the color of the pigment/lemon juice mixture. If the colors are the same, then the pH of the precipitation is the same as that of lemon juice. To get a more accurate reading, check with your science teacher for some universal pH paper. Use this paper to measure the pH of the precipitation. How do the pH readings obtained with the cabbage solution and the pH paper compare? Why might they be different?

You can easily see how acid precipitation affects marble structures such as statues and buildings. Place some seashells in a glass and cover them with vinegar. The seashells contain calcium carbonate, the same chemical compound that is in marble. What happens to the seashells in vinegar? How are marble structures affected by acid precipitation?

Project Idea

Tracking Acid Precipitation

Design a project that tracks acid precipitation in your local community over time. Use a computer at school or home to locate someone who is willing to set up a similar tracking program in another part of the country. Compare your findings. Determine if the rain is more acidic during certain times of the year, times of the day, or at the beginning versus the end of a rainfall. Search the Internet to find out what federal, state, and local officials have done to control acid precipitation. Check to see whether your community has taken any action to combat the effects of acid precipitation. If they have, find out and report what they have done.

Experiment 3.4

Which Color(s) Do Plants Prefer for Photosynthesis?

Materials

* elodea plants
* 12 test tubes
* 3 test tube holders
* water
* 3 light sources
* colored filters
* one-hole rubber stopper
* rubber tubing
* short piece of plastic or glass tubing
* small plastic syringe
* food dye

Life as we know it would not be possible without **photosynthesis**. The fruits and vegetables in a supermarket are the products of plants that have carried out photosynthesis. Photosynthesis is the process by which plants take in carbon dioxide gas and water and convert them into sugar and oxygen gas. The sugars plants produce are the basis of all the nutrients that living things take in to survive. The oxygen plants produce is used by living things, including plants, to carry out respiration.

To conduct photosynthesis, plants require two things: light, which they usually get from the sun, and chlorophyll, the pigment that gives them their green color. The sunlight provides the energy, which is trapped by the chlorophyll for use by the plants to keep photosynthesis operating.

You know that sunlight is white. You probably know that this white light is actually made up of several different colors. You can easily see this for yourself by observing a rainbow or by passing white light through a prism. Is there a color of light that is better for photosynthesis, or do plants carry out photosynthesis to the same extent regardless of the color light that is used? You can carry out this experiment to determine the answer.

Elodea is a freshwater plant that can be found in pet stores, where it is sold under the name Anacharis. Set up 12 test tubes, each containing the same-size piece of elodea. Fill the test tubes with water to cover the plants. Why is it important that all the elodea plants be the same size and that the volume of water in each test tube be the same?

Divide your test tubes equally into three groups. Expose each group to a different color of light. To get red light, cover the light source with a red filter. If you do not have colored filters, you can cover the light source with colored plastic used to wrap foods. Expose another group to blue light, and a third group to green light.

Recall that plants produce oxygen during photosynthesis. Thus the higher the rate of photosynthesis, the more oxygen produced. Look for the oxygen gas bubbles released by the plants. Which plants produce the most oxygen gas? A more accurate way to compare the rates of photosynthesis is to use a manometer. A **manometer** is a device that measures the pressure exerted by a gas or liquid. All manometers operate on the same principle, as you can see in Figure 15.

You can make a U-shaped manometer out of glass or plastic tubing. Be sure that the diameter of the tubing is narrow. Fill the tubing partially with a colored fluid, such as a food dye added to water. Connect one end of the tubing to a sealed test tube containing a plant carrying out photosynthesis. Connect the other end to a small plastic syringe. Oxygen gas produced by the plant will force the liquid to move. The

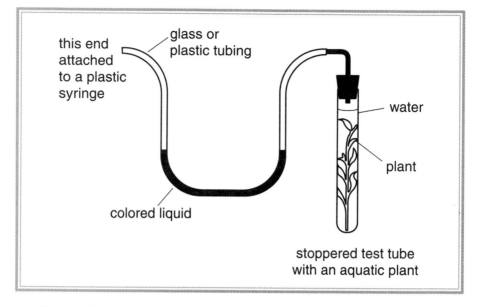

Figure 15. A manometer can be used to measure the volume of oxygen gas given off by a plant during photosynthesis.

volume of oxygen gas that replaced the colored liquid can be determined by using the syringe. The volume of oxygen gas corresponds to the volume of air in the syringe that is used to force the colored liquid back to its original position. Record the original and final positions of the syringe plunger. The difference between these two values represents the volume of oxygen gas produced by the plants that caused the fluid in the tube to move.

Once you have your manometer working, you can check how other factors affect photosynthesis. You can vary how much carbon dioxide the plants get by placing them in different concentrations of a sodium bicarbonate (baking soda) solution. You can also vary the intensity of light by using light-bulbs with different watts or by changing the distance between the plants and the light source.

Experiment 3.5

Is Green the Only Pigment in Plants?

Now you can turn your attention from the colors outside a plant to those inside a plant. A quick look at the vegetable section in a supermarket would confirm something that you know—plants are green. But is that the only color that you can find inside a plant? The next time you are in a supermarket, buy some spinach to use in this experiment.

Because alcohol is very flammable, **have an adult boil the spinach** in isopropyl (rubbing) alcohol. However, ethyl alcohol works better. Because ethyl alcohol is commonly used in a school laboratory, you can ask your science teacher for permission to carry out this step, using ethyl alcohol in class. The adult should continue to boil the spinach until the solution is a very dark green.

Cut a piece of filter paper and use a paper clip to suspend it in a glass, as shown in Figure 16. A thick coffee filter will also work. But check with your science teacher to see whether it is possible to get some chromatography paper to use in place of filter paper. Remove the paper from the glass and use a toothpick to draw a thin, dark line of the green solution about 4 cm from the bottom of the paper. Allow the solution to dry.

Materials

* spinach
* an adult
* rubbing alcohol
* small pot
* stove
* thick filter paper or thick coffee filter
* large paper clip
* large drinking glass
* toothpick
* metric ruler

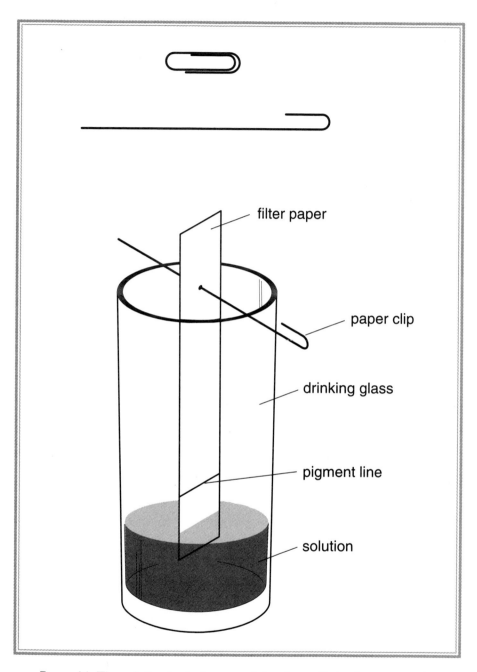

Figure 16. The solution in the bottom of the glass will slowly move up the paper. Each component in a mixture that has been placed on the paper has a different attraction for the solution. Thus, each component will travel up the paper at a different rate. As a result, the various components in a mixture will be separated.

Then draw another thin line on top of the first one. Allow this second line to dry; then apply a third one. Repeat this procedure until you have a dark line. In this way, you will have applied a lot of pigment to the paper.

Pour rubbing alcohol into the glass to a depth of 2 cm. Use the paper clip to suspend the filter paper in the alcohol. Make sure that the level of the alcohol in the glass is below the dark green line, as shown in Figure 16. If not, pour out some of the alcohol. Allow the alcohol to move up the filter paper. Do not disturb the glass. Remove the filter paper when the alcohol approaches the paper clip.

Examine the paper after it has dried. What do your results tell you about the colors present in a plant? Repeat this process using various vegetables that an adult has boiled in alcohol. How well the various pigments are separated depends in part on the solution in which the paper is placed. Experiment with different solutions. In addition to rubbing alcohol, try vinegar, water, or other solutions that your science teacher has available. Be sure to **check with an adult** before using a different solution to separate the pigments in a plant. Also try different combinations by mixing any two or even three of these solutions. Vary the proportions of the solutions you mix.

Project Idea

Chromatography

The process of separating the various colored pigments in a solution is known as **chromatography**. For obvious reasons, the process you used is called paper chromatography. At one time, this was the only type of chromatography available to scientists. Today, however, scientists can use liquid chromatography and gas chromatography to separate the components that may be present in a mixture. Search the Internet for information about how these processes are done and what information they can provide to scientists. Another key phrase to use in your search is high pressure liquid chromatography (HPLC).

Chances are that none of these chromatography processes are available at your school. But you may want to contact a local university or research facility to see whether they have the equipment to carry out either HPLC, or liquid or gas chromatography. Perhaps you may be able to observe how they operate and even help in the process.

Experiment 3.6

Why Do Plants Wilt?

Have you ever noticed a sprinkler system come on in a supermarket? If you have, hopefully it was not the one used to put out fires but rather the one used in the vegetable section. Periodically, the system comes on and sprays the produce with water. If vegetables were not kept

Materials
* 2 celery stalks
* 2 glasses
* water
* refrigerator

moist, chances are people would not buy them because of the way they would look. Without enough water, vegetables will wilt because of a lack of turgor pressure.

Turgor pressure is the pressure that water exerts inside a plant cell. As you can see in Figure 17, a plant cell is surrounded by two structures. One structure is called a **cell membrane**. The second structure surrounds the cell membrane and is known as a **cell wall**. All cells have a cell membrane, but only plant cells have a cell wall. Unlike a cell membrane, a cell wall is rigid. As water moves into a plant cell, it pushes the cell membrane against the cell wall, creating a force known as turgor pressure. Turgor pressure keeps the cell walls stiff and the plants crisp.

Place one stalk of celery in a glass and the other stalk in a glass half filled with water. Refrigerate both glasses and observe what happens to the celery stalks over the next several days. Which one would you buy in a supermarket? Eat for dinner? Give to friends? Account for any differences in the appearance of the celery stalks. Explain your observations in terms of

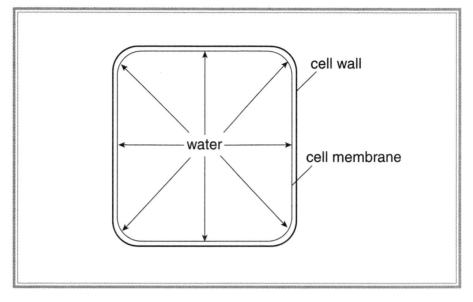

Figure 17. As a plant cell fills with water, the water pushes against the cell membrane, which in turn pushes against the cell wall. This results in turgor pressure.

turgor pressure. Now do you know why they keep the vegetables moistened in a supermarket?

Unlike plant cells, animal cells do not exhibit turgor pressure. Animal cells are not surrounded by a cell wall. If too much water enters an animal cell, the water will push against the cell membrane. Without a cell wall to hold the water back, the cell will burst. This can be a deadly problem for animals that live in freshwater. Fortunately, their cells have ways of getting rid of any excess water that enters.

Project Idea

Turgor Pressure

Check with your science teacher for permission to use a microscope to carry out a project investigating turgor pressure in an aquatic plant. Change the environmental conditions to see what happens to plant cells in terms of their turgor pressure. Independent variables that you can change include the salt concentration of the water, lighting conditions, and carbon dioxide concentration. You can also investigate the role that turgor pressure plays in thigmonastic movements. These are movements that plants demonstrate in response to touching or shaking. Perhaps you are familiar with a well-known example—the folding of the leaves of a Venus flytrap in response to touch.

Experiment 3.7

What Is Inside a Seed?

Many people like to eat fruit. But few people know what they are eating when they consume a strawberry, orange, banana, or grapefruit. Scientists define a fruit as a matured ovary. If you think about this definition, it makes sense. Fruits usually contain seeds. Seeds can be planted to produce new plants. Thus the fruit must be involved in some way in the reproduction of a plant.

In plants, an **ovary** is the female reproductive structure that is located

Materials

* bean seeds
* corn kernels
* water
* small glass
* an adult
* single-edge razor blade
* magnifying glass
* Lugol's iodine

at the base of a flower. The pollen of a plant contains sperm cells, which travel down the flower to fertilize an egg cell inside an **ovule**. An ovule is a special type of cell that forms inside the ovary. Each fertilized ovule develops into a seed. Following fertilization, the ovary surrounding the seeds matures and enlarges to form a fruit. When you eat fruit, seeds are just a nuisance. You spit them out and toss them into the garbage. But did you ever stop to think about what is inside that little seed you threw away? Here is your chance to find out.

Soak some bean seeds and corn kernels in water for 30 minutes. Remove the covering that surrounds the bean seeds. This is known as the seed coat. **With the help of an adult**, use a razor blade to cut open some bean seeds. In the case of the corn kernel, use a magnifying lens to locate the small, oval, light-colored area that shows through the seed coat. Use a razor blade to cut the corn kernel in half along the length of this area. Compare what you see in the seeds with what is shown in Figure 18. A stereomicroscope will help you see the structures more clearly. Check with your science teacher to see whether such a microscope is available for you to use. Draw each seed and label all the parts you can identify.

Also check with your science teacher for some Lugol's iodine. Soak the cut surface of each seed in a few drops of Lugol's iodine. This solution stains starch a blue-black color. Lugol's iodine will also stain your hands and clothes, so be careful when using it. How much of each seed is starch? What purpose does this starch serve in the seed?

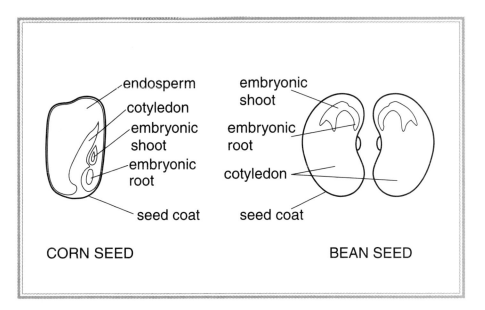

Figure 18. The seed coat is a protective layer. The endosperm in the corn is stored food for the seed to grow. The cotyledons also store food for the corn and bean seeds. Find the only parts that will develop into the adult plant—the embryonic shoot and root.

Project Idea

Hydroponics

Seeds need only water and oxygen to germinate, or start growing. They do not need soil. The growth of plants without soil is known as **hydroponics**. You can observe hydroponics by wrapping some seeds in a paper towel that is secured with a rubber band. Place the paper towel upright in water, making sure that the seeds are above the level of the water. Check the seeds periodically to observe their progress. Experiment with ways of speeding up germination and growth. For example, you can add various nutrients to the water. Also search the Internet for progress being made with hydroponics as a way of increasing food production.

Experiment 3.8

Why Is Making a Pineapple Gelatin Dessert Not a Good Idea?

Life depends on chemical reactions. For example, the human body could not survive without the chemical reactions that make up digestion, respiration, and excretion. In fact, the human body can be considered a chemical factory in which numerous chemical reactions take place. But these chemical reactions would not take place without the help of enzymes. An **enzyme** is a chemical substance that speeds up the rate of a reaction. Enzymes are involved in the transport of carbon dioxide in the blood, in the production of waste materials, and in the digestion of foods.

Some enzymes are involved in the digestion of fats, a group of organic compounds that you read about in Chapter 2. Other enzymes help digest the two other kinds of organic compounds found in foods—carbohydrates and proteins. Like fats, both carbohydrates and proteins contain the elements carbon, hydrogen, and oxygen. A **carbohydrate** is characterized by having a carbon:hydrogen:oxygen ratio of 1:2:1. For example, $C_6H_{12}O_6$, the formula for the sugar made by plants in photosynthesis, is a carbohydrate. A **protein** is characterized by having the element nitrogen as part of its chemical makeup. In this experiment, you can explore how enzymes can digest a gelatin dessert, which is mostly protein.

Follow the instructions on the package to prepare a gelatin dessert. While you are enjoying some of the gelatin, take a small chunk and place it on a clean dish. Place a slice of pineapple on top of the gelatin and observe what happens. Now you should realize why adding fresh pineapple to a gelatin dessert is not a good idea.

As the proteins are digested by enzymes, they are broken into smaller compounds. As these smaller compounds form, the solid gelatin turns into a liquid. Does pineapple have the same effect on carbohydrates? You can check this out by placing a slice of pineapple on a cut potato, which is mostly carbohydrate. Also check to see whether the way fruit is prepared makes a difference. Observe what happens whether you use frozen, cooked, canned, or dried pineapple in place of fresh pineapple. Try other fruits, such as an apple, grapefruit, cantaloupe, or pear, to see whether they have the same effect on proteins.

Chapter 4

Meat Products

One aisle in a supermarket where shoppers frequently stop to look is the meat section. The only exceptions might be people with a stockpile of meat in a big freezer at home and people who do not eat meat. But for everyone else, shopping at a supermarket probably means sorting through the beef, chicken, pork, veal, and lamb products. Even these shoppers, however, often bypass one meat product—liver. You probably understand why. After all, liver is something that very few people eat.

The next time you go shopping at the supermarket, however, be sure to buy some liver—not for a meal but for an experiment. If you feel like it, though, you can volunteer to cook the liver for your family dinner someday. This meal is really simple to prepare. Just dip the liver in flour, fry it in a little oil, and serve it with fried onions and a baked potato.

Experiment 4.1

What Can You Do with Liver Besides Eat It?

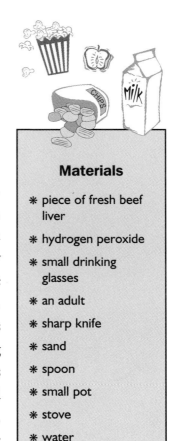

Materials

* piece of fresh beef liver
* hydrogen peroxide
* small drinking glasses
* an adult
* sharp knife
* sand
* spoon
* small pot
* stove
* water

The liver is a most interesting organ. As you might gather from Figure 19, the liver is the largest internal organ in the human body. Weighing nearly 1.5 kg (slightly more than 3 lbs), the liver is about the size of a football. This large size reflects the many jobs it performs in the body. Among other things, the liver makes proteins, stores vitamins and minerals, regulates blood clotting, and eliminates alcohol and poisons from the body. To carry out so many functions, the liver is provided with a rich blood supply. You can easily demonstrate this for yourself by holding a piece of fresh beef liver in your hand. Put it down and then look at your hand. Although you may think that what you see is disgusting, the blood in liver provides an opportunity for you to carry out an interesting experiment.

Under adult supervision use a sharp knife to cut or chop up the liver. Take a small piece of liver and place it in a glass. By the way, you can substitute a potato for the liver, but it is not as much fun to watch what happens. Cover the liver with hydrogen peroxide and observe what happens. Clean out the glass. Take a piece of liver the same size as before, but this time chop it into the smallest pieces possible. Place the chopped liver in the glass. Cover the liver with hydrogen peroxide and observe what happens.

To chop the liver, you can also add a small amount of sand to a piece of liver and then crush it with a spoon. This will really grind the liver into small pieces. Add a small amount of hydrogen peroxide and watch what happens. Next, boil a piece

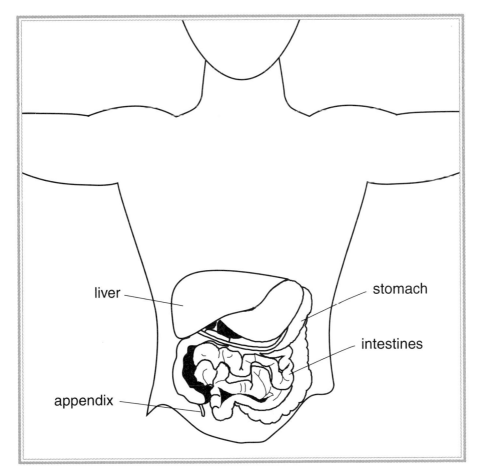

Figure 19. The liver extends across the body. It makes proteins, stores vitamins, and eliminates poisons from the body.

of liver in water. Allow the liver to cool, place it in the glass, and cover it with hydrogen peroxide. What happens when you boil the liver?

Hydrogen peroxide is an unstable compound and will slowly break down, especially when it is exposed to light. Now you know why hydrogen peroxide is stored in an opaque container. Even in the presence of light, however, the breakdown of hydrogen peroxide is a slow process.

The blood in liver contains an enzyme called catalase. You read in Chapter 3 that an enzyme is a substance that speeds up a chemical reaction. Catalase speeds up the breakdown of hydrogen peroxide. When hydrogen peroxide is broken down, oxygen gas and water are produced. The bubbles you observed in your experiment were oxygen gas bubbles. Breaking the liver into small pieces exposes more enzymes to the hydrogen peroxide. Thus the reaction occurs even faster. Excessive heat destroys enzymes. Now you know why no bubbles were produced when you used boiled liver.

By the way, you may have poured a little hydrogen peroxide on a small cut you once got. Perhaps you noticed all the small bubbles that were produced near the cut. Catalase in your blood breaks down the hydrogen peroxide. The oxygen that was produced helps kill bacteria that might otherwise cause an infection. Certain bacteria do not function well when exposed to oxygen. In fact, they may die.

Project Idea

Testing for Iron

Liver is rich in iron. Iron is one chemical that is often used as a food fortifier. Usually added to breakfast cereals and breads, iron is needed to make hemoglobin. Hemoglobin, a protein that is found in red blood cells, transports oxygen to the cells where it is used for producing the energy the body requires. Without sufficient iron, red blood cells could not supply the cells with enough oxygen. The result would be a disease known as **anemia**, which is characterized by a lack of energy.

You can easily test for iron in breakfast cereals. Just mix some cereal with water in a clear bowl. Take a large magnet and pass it back and forth across the bottom of the bowl, as shown in Figure 20. If iron is present, you should see black iron filings, which are attracted to the magnet, collect at the bottom of the bowl. Testing for iron in other foods is not as easy. One way is to use a chemical called potassium thiocyanate. **Be sure to carry out this procedure, which involves the use of a strong acid, under the supervision of your science teacher.** Potassium thiocyanate reacts with iron in the presence of a strong acid to produce a red color. The more iron present, the darker the red color.

Your science teacher should help you develop a specific procedure. The basic framework of this project follows. You must first pulverize a food sample. The sample is then heated, usually in a small container called a crucible, until only an ash residue remains. When the crucible has cooled, the ash is transferred to a clean beaker and mixed with 10 mL of distilled water. Any iron present in the ash will dissolve in the water. The solution is filtered, and the filtrate is collected in a clean beaker. The **filtrate** is the liquid that passes through the filter. A few drops of concentrated nitric acid are added to the filtrate followed by 2 mL of 0.1M potassium thiocyanate solution. The *M* refers to the concentration of the solution. If iron is present in the solution, a red color will develop.

Before testing various foods, you may want to test your procedure with vitamin tablets that contain iron. Be sure to soak the tablets in water to dissolve any colored coating so that it does not interfere with your test. If you use the potassium thiocyanate procedure, you do not have to worry about the color of foods you test, such as liver, because you will heat them until only an ash residue remains.

Figure 20. Any iron filings in the cereal will be attracted to the magnet as it is passed under the bowl. Because the iron filings are small and scattered throughout the cereal, it will take some time before they collect near the bottom of the bowl.

Experiment 4.2

How Do You Soften a Tough Piece of Beef?

Materials

* gelatin
* meat tenderizer
* 2 saucers
* straw

Undoubtedly, you have eaten a tough piece of beef. If you knew that the meat was tough before it was cooked, some meat tenderizer could have been sprinkled on it. Did you ever wonder what meat tenderizer actually does to soften meat? Try the following experiment to see what tenderizer does to protein, which is the main component of meat. You use gelatin rather than meat, because the effect is easier to observe. In fact, this experiment is very similar to the one in Experiment 3.8 where fresh fruit was placed on top of gelatin.

Prepare some gelatin. Divide the gelatin into two pieces. Place each piece on a saucer. Sprinkle some meat tenderizer on one piece until there is a thin layer covering the gelatin. Allow the two pieces to remain undisturbed for five to ten minutes. Then gently poke the gelatin pieces with a straw. Explain your observations.

Think back to Experiment 3.8. What was present in the fresh fruit that caused the gelatin to liquefy? What must be present in meat tenderizer? Why is it advisable to allow especially tough meat and tenderizer to stand for a few hours before broiling or barbecuing the meat? Test other household products such as vinegar and lemon juice for their ability to tenderize proteins.

Experiment 4.3

Where's the Beef?

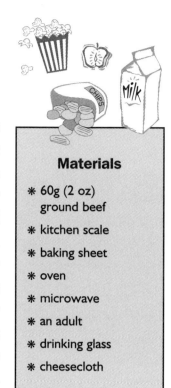

Materials

* 60g (2 oz) ground beef
* kitchen scale
* baking sheet
* oven
* microwave
* an adult
* drinking glass
* cheesecloth

Beef tastes good because of the fats it contains. However, too much fat is not only unhealthy but also responsible for giving foods a greasy taste. The amount of fat permitted in certain foods is regulated by law. For example, the maximum for ground beef is 30 percent, and that for lean beef is 15 percent. How does the beef in your supermarket compare with these figures? The following experiment will give you the answer. But be warned. This experiment could stink up your kitchen.

Weigh 60 g (about 2 oz) of uncooked ground beef. Spread the beef out on a baking sheet and, **under adult supervision**, place it in the oven for 30 minutes at 220°. The heat will evaporate the water in the meat. Allow the meat to cool. Remove the meat from the tray and weigh it. Subtract the weight of the dehydrated meat from the weight of the uncooked meat. The difference represents the weight of the water in the original meat sample.

Place the dehydrated meat in a piece of cheesecloth. Suspend the cheesecloth over a glass, as shown in Figure 21. Place the glass and the meat in a microwave. Microwave the meat until it looks dry and shriveled. The microwave will extract the fat from the meat. Some of the fat will collect as a

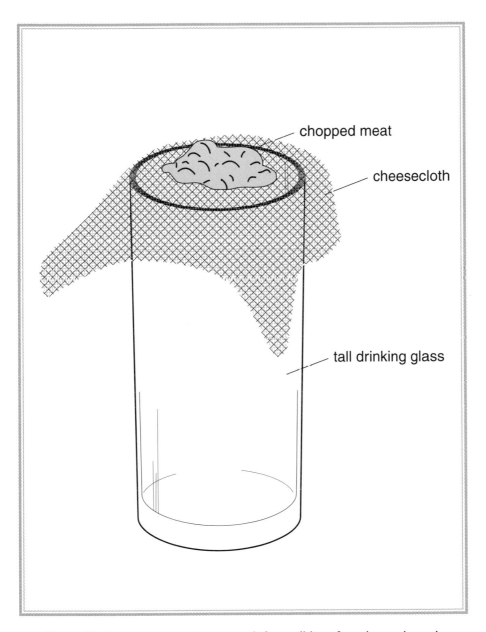

chopped meat

cheesecloth

tall drinking glass

Figure 21. As the meat is microwaved, fats will liquefy and pass through the cheesecloth into the glass. The high heat may vaporize some of the fats, producing a foul smell.

liquid in the glass. The rest will be vaporized. If possible, you may want to do this step outside on a deck or patio so that the vapors do not make the kitchen smell bad.

Allow the meat to cool, remove it from the cheesecloth, and weigh it. Subtract the weight of the microwaved meat from the weight of the dehydrated meat. This represents the mass of the fat in the original meat sample. Determine the percent of fat in your meat sample by using the following formula.

$$\frac{\text{weight of fat}}{\text{weight of dehydrated meat}} \times 100 = \text{percent fat}$$

Once you know how much water and fat are in meat, you may wonder where the beef is. Keep in mind that this procedure will give you only a rough idea of the fat content of meat. Using a microwave is not the best way to extract the fats from meat. To obtain a more accurate value of the fat content of meat, carry out the following project.

Project Idea

How to Spot a Fat Hamburger or Hot Dog

Extracting the fat from meat is possible if you do what chemists do—use a solvent. Because fats and water do not mix, you must use a solvent that will dissolve the grease. Such a solvent must be nonpolar and organic, like fats. Recall the expression from Experiment 2.4 that "like dissolves like." Hexane is a good solvent to use to determine the fat content of a wide variety of beef products, including fast-food hamburgers and hot dogs. When mixed with meat, hexane will dissolve the fats that are present. The hexane can then be evaporated, leaving the fats.

Be sure to carry out this project under a teacher's supervision. Weigh out a meat sample; 25 g is a good quantity to use. Chop the meat into the smallest pieces possible and cover them with hexane. Do not use hexane near any flames because it is flammable. Because hexane also evaporates fairly quickly and produces an odor, use a fume hood.

You should stir the meat and hexane as thoroughly as possible for 15 to 20 minutes. You can then filter everything through cheesecloth to collect the hexane. The hexane will have a yellowish color because of the fats that it contains. Collect the hexane in a clean container that you have weighed. A large, broad container, such as the one shown in Figure 22, is good to use because you want a large surface area to speed up the evaporation process. The hexane will slowly evaporate, leaving the fats in the container as a solid mass. Placing the container in the fume hood at school will speed up the process. Weighing the container after all the hexane has evaporated will allow you to calculate how much fat you extracted. Dividing this value by the mass of the meat will give you the percent fat.

While you have your meat samples, you may also want to check out their water content. Follow the procedure for evaporating the water as described in Experiment 4.3. Your results will tell you what is meant by a "juicy frank."

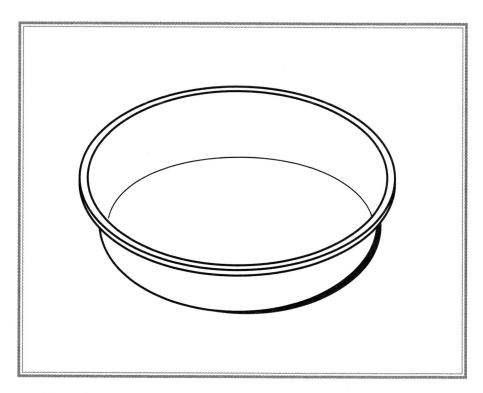

Figure 22. Scientists use an evaporating dish when they want to allow a liquid to evaporate. The wide surface area allows the liquid to evaporate more quickly. Any solid materials will be left behind in the dish.

Project Idea

The Cost of Raising Beef

Concerns have recently been raised about the environmental cost of raising beef. Much has been made about fast-food franchises buying their meat for hamburger patties from South American farmers. These farmers have burned down large tracts of tropical rain forests to obtain pasturelands to graze their cattle. In response to such concerns, these franchises now purchase much of their beef from steers that are grazed on farms in the Midwest. Nonetheless, environmentalists are still concerned.

About 60 percent of the corn grown in the United States goes to feed the livestock that will eventually become beef for the supermarket. Scientists estimate that growing the corn for just one pound of beef results in the erosion of a little more than four pounds of topsoil. Growing one acre of corn requires 640,000 gallons of water, causing an enormous drain on this natural resource. Prepare a report that summarizes the overall impact on our environment caused by raising the beef and chicken that are sold by fast-food franchises. You can also research the impact resulting from the growing of potatoes that they use for the French fries.

Experiment 4.4

Why Do Bones Sometimes Break So Easily?

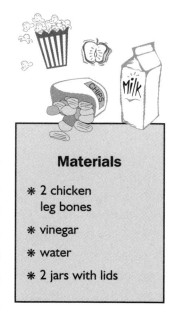

Materials

* 2 chicken leg bones

* vinegar

* water

* 2 jars with lids

The next time you have chicken for dinner, save the bones. Examine a leg bone. Notice how light the bone is. Carefully snap the bone into two pieces. A soft material called bone marrow fills the spaces inside the bone. Marrow also fills the spaces in your bones. Some of this marrow is called *red marrow*, which produces red blood cells in some bones. The hollow interiors of your leg and arm bones are filled with *yellow marrow*, which stores fats. If you extracted the fats from beef, can you tell how yellow marrow got its name? Whether they contain red marrow or yellow marrow, bones are not easy to break. You may have discovered this when you tried to break open your chicken bone. But under certain conditions bones can break easily. This experiment will show you the reason.

Place a chicken bone in each jar. Cover the bone in one jar with vinegar and the other bone with water. Place the lids on the jars. Place the jars in a cabinet. After several days, pour off the vinegar and rinse the bone with running water. Remove the bone soaked in water. Bend the bones. Observe what happens.

The acid in the vinegar dissolves the substance that makes bones hard. This substance is calcium phosphate. Without calcium phosphate, bones lose their hardness and become more brittle or likely to break.

Project Ideas

Osteoporosis

Bones are continually broken down and replaced with new bone. In babies, new bone is added more rapidly than it is broken down, so the bones get larger. Once the baby becomes a young adult, new bone is added at the same rate that it is broken down. During middle age, the rate at which bone is broken down is greater than that at which new bone is formed. As a result, the bones do not contain as much calcium phosphate and can break more easily. If the bone loss is severe, the condition is called **osteoporosis**. In the United States, more than 600,000 fractures result from osteoporosis each year.

Calcium supplements are recommended for people, especially women, who are at the age when osteoporosis can start to develop. Search the Internet for information about osteoporosis. Prepare a report that answers the following questions: Why are women more likely to develop osteoporosis? What can be done besides taking calcium supplements to combat osteoporosis? At what age should a person start taking steps to prevent developing osteoporosis? What role does vitamin D play in bone development?

Checking for Bacteria

To cut down on their blood cholesterol levels, people often avoid red meats in favor of white meats, especially chicken. But these meats have periodically raised consumer concerns for other reasons. Chickens, and the eggs hens lay, have been known to be contaminated with bacteria that can cause food poisoning. Several food-poisoning bacteria commonly infect chickens. The best-known one is *Salmonella*. Approximately two thousand different types of

Salmonella have been identified. You can carry out a project that checks for the presence of bacteria growing on a number of different things, including chicken. **Be sure that you carry out this project under the supervision of a science teacher**.

First, you will need to learn some techniques in microbiology. **Microbiology** is the study of tiny living things, such as bacteria, that are too small to be seen without a microscope. Specifically you will need to learn how to culture or grow microorganisms in round containers called petri dishes. A substance called agar is added to the petri dish to provide a solid surface on which the bacteria can grow. Nutrients are first mixed with the agar so that the bacteria can live and reproduce. Different types of agar/nutrient petri dishes can be prepared or purchased, depending on the type of bacteria that is being studied.

The procedure is straightforward. Use a sterile swab to wipe the surface of a piece of chicken. Then wipe the swab over the surface of the agar. The dish is incubated at a temperature best suited for the bacteria to thrive and reproduce. Room temperature is often satisfactory. It may just take a little longer for the bacteria to become visible, like those shown in Figure 23. When a petri dish is no longer needed, the agar should be covered with liquid bleach to destroy the bacteria. The dishes should be soaked with bleach for 24 hours and then carefully washed with running water.

Care must also be taken not to come in contact with any bacteria that appear on the petri dishes. You never know what kinds of bacteria are growing on the dishes. Some may be able to produce a disease. Thus this project should definitely be done **under adult supervision**, and the petri dishes should be kept in a secure place that no one else has access to.

Your project should also examine the effect of washing

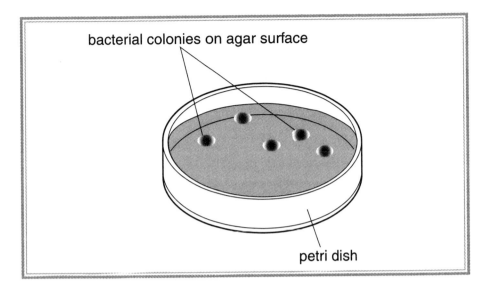

bacterial colonies on agar surface

petri dish

Figure 23. The circular areas on the surface of the agar represent colonies of bacteria. Each colony consists of millions of bacterial cells that have been produced from just one bacterial cell that was originally on the agar.

the chicken before it is cooked. Is the number of bacteria significantly reduced after washing? How does cooking affect the number of bacteria? Tell everyone at dinner the next time you have chicken to wait before they start eating. Then go around the dinner table taking your sterile samples for analysis. Expand your project to check on what is being done to reduce the number of bacteria in food-processing plants. A recent report indicated that the use of electropolished steel in chicken-processing equipment greatly reduced the number of bacteria. You can use your newly learned microbiology techniques to test anything for its bacteria content. Another recent report revealed that sponges, rags, and sinks in homes are contaminated with bacteria. How clean are the ones in your home?

Pork

Everyone realizes that pork must be thoroughly cooked. If pork is pink when cut, it should not be eaten. Instead, the meat should be cooked some more until it has a uniform grayish-white color. The concern about undercooked pork is trichinosis. **Trichinosis** is a disease caused by a microscopic organism that can live in humans or animals. This microscopic organism is the roundworm. When humans eat an animal infected with this roundworm, they in turn become infected.

The roundworms penetrate into the intestine where they thrive and reproduce. Newly produced roundworms are carried by the blood to other parts of the body, especially the muscles, where they can survive for a long time. Symptoms of a trichinosis infection include fever, muscle soreness, thirst, chills, and pain and swelling around the eyes. Failure to treat the disease can result in death. But fortunately there is a drug that can kill the roundworm.

Very few people today develop trichinosis. In 1989, the Centers for Disease Control in Atlanta, Georgia, reported fewer than 50 cases of trichinosis in the United States. In 1950, there were nearly 500 cases reported. The decrease in trichinosis cases can be attributed to several reasons. The United States Department of Agriculture requires meat plants to heat processed meats to at least 137°F before sale. This temperature kills any roundworms that may be present. In addition, hogs are no longer fed uncooked food wastes as they were in the past. Such food wastes contained the roundworm that infected these animals. When humans ate these hogs, they in turn became infected.

Project Idea

Irradiated Foods

Recently, meat processors have started to irradiate pork products to kill any roundworms that may be present. The Food and Drug Administration approved this method to treat pork in 1985, some sixty years after it was first used on foods. But just the word *irradiation* raises concerns for some people.

Check out your local supermarket to see whether it sells any irradiated foods. If so, how are they labeled? Prepare a report on irradiated foods. Be sure to include information about the science behind the irradiation process. What type of radiation is used? How does radiation kill roundworms and other potentially harmful organisms in food? What "doses" are used for different foods? Why is pork given less radiation than strawberries? Where is the process carried out in the United States? How does the use of radiation on foods in the United States compare with its use in other countries? Why do some hospitals irradiate the foods they feed certain patients?

If you can, buy some irradiated strawberries. Invite your friends over for a taste test. Have them compare the taste of irradiated strawberries with ones that have not been irradiated. Strawberries are irradiated to prolong their shelf life. As part of your project, determine how much longer irradiated strawberries last without spoiling.

Chapter 5

Snacks, Desserts, and Candies

Your favorite aisles at a supermarket are likely the ones with the snack foods, desserts, and candies. In fact, these aisles are probably the favorite ones for many people. Most everyone can recall a day when they devoured a large container of popcorn at the movies, downed a whole bag of pretzels at a picnic, or ate a bowl of potato chips while watching television. Although these snack foods may satisfy our hunger, they provide only limited quantities of a few important nutrients. Moreover, if a person maintained a steady diet of these foods, the extra pounds would quickly begin to show. The same is true not only of snack foods but also desserts and candies. The increased weight would result from the large number of calories present in these foods.

A calorie is the unit scientists use to

measure the energy content of foods. One **calorie** is defined as the quantity of energy that is required to raise the temperature of 1 gram of water 1°C. Be careful not to confuse this calorie with the one you see written on the labels of food products. The calorie content of foods as reported on the label is not the same as the calorie used by scientists. To avoid confusion, the scientific version should be written with a lowercase "c" (calorie), whereas the dietetic version should be written with an uppercase "C" (Calorie). One Calorie actually equals 1,000 calories. This distinction, however, is not always clear. The next time you have a can of soda in your hands, check the label. If it is not a diet soda, it may say that one serving contains 100 *calories*. But that is actually 100 *Calories* or 100,000 *calories*. One snack food that contains a lot of calories, no matter how you spell it, is a potato chip.

Experiment 5.1

How Many Calories Does One Potato Chip Contain?

Materials

* ✶ large metal can
* ✶ metal shears
* ✶ hammer
* ✶ large nail
* ✶ aluminum foil
* ✶ water
* ✶ measuring cup
* ✶ metric ruler
* ✶ matches
* ✶ thermometer
* ✶ baby food jars
* ✶ potato chips
* ✶ an adult

The first potato chip came about as a result of a practical joke. In 1854, a wealthy American named Cornelius Vanderbilt was dining at a restaurant in Saratoga Springs, New York. When his meal was served, he was not happy with the way his fried potatoes looked. He thought they were too thick and ordered the waiter to take them back to the kitchen. The chef was annoyed and decided to retaliate. He cut paper-thin slices of potatoes and then fried them to a crisp in hot oil. Little did the chef suspect what would happen next. When he was served his fried potatoes this time, Vanderbilt loved them. Potato chips had been created and would soon become a huge success. Now that you know how potato chips were first made, the next time you open a bag, save a few for an experiment. In that way, you will also save a few calories.

Use a large metal can to construct a calorimeter, as shown in Figure 24. A coffee can or any other large, metal container would be suitable. Remove the top. **Ask an adult** to use a metal shears to cut out a wedge along one edge. Invert the can so that

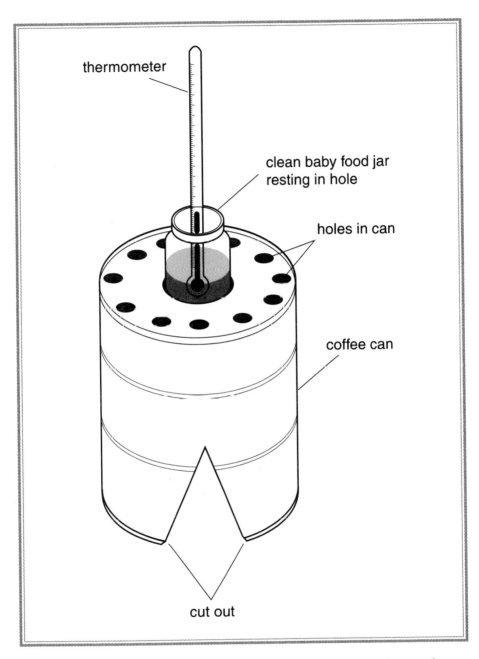

thermometer

clean baby food jar
resting in hole

holes in can

coffee can

cut out

Figure 24. You can use a large metal can to construct a calorimeter. As
the food sample underneath the glass jar burns, the temperature of the
water inside the jar rises. Why would wrapping the metal can and the
glass jar in aluminum foil be a good idea?

the bottom is upright. Carefully cut a hole in the bottom, wide enough to hold a small baby food jar. Be sure that the hole is large enough to hold the jar but not too large so that it falls through the hole. If you have made the hole too large, wrap the jar with aluminum foil to get a tight fit. Use a hammer and a large nail to punch several air holes around this opening.

Place the baby food jar in the hole. Pour 30 mL (approximately 1 fluid ounce) of water into the jar. Place a thermometer into the jar and record the water temperature. Then make a small "frying pan" out of a sheet of aluminum foil. Place the potato chip in the frying pan. You will have to rig up something so that the potato chip rests about 2 cm (1 in) below the bottom of the baby food jar in the can. You might place the frying pan with its potato chip on another baby food jar or a small glass.

Remove your calorimeter and **ask an adult** to ignite the potato chip with a match. It should burn fairly easily because of the oils it contains, but they may have to try lighting it more than once. If your potato chip does not ignite, try another one. Once the chip is burning, carefully place your calorimeter over it. Be sure that the bottom of the baby food jar does not extinguish the flame. After the potato chip has completely burned, observe the thermometer and record the highest temperature of the water.

As the potato chip burns, heat energy is transferred to the water. To calculate the number of calories in the chip, place your data into the following equation.

calories = volume of water x (final water temperature−initial water temperature)

For example, if the temperature of the water inside the baby jar went from 22°C to 68°C, then you would get the following result.

$$\text{calories} = 30 \times (68-22) = 30 \times 46 = 1{,}380 \text{ calories}$$

Notice that the formula uses volume of water, while calorie was defined in terms of the mass of water that is used in the calorimeter. At most temperatures, 1 g of water equals approximately 1 mL of water. Thus, you can substitute the volume of water in the equation for calculating calories. But the volume must be in mL. If your measuring device is marked in fluid ounces, then use the following formula to convert.

$$946 \text{ mL} = 32 \text{ fluid ounces}$$

How many calories did your potato chip contain? How many Calories? Check a reference source in your school library or on the Internet to see how many calories are recommended daily for someone your age, sex, height, weight, and degree of activity. How many potato chips would you have to eat in a day to obtain that number of calories? You can repeat this experiment, this time using a peanut or a walnut to determine its calorie content. No matter what you use, why is your calorimeter not as accurate as it could be? To determine the actual calorie content of a food sample, scientists use an insulated calorimeter where an electrical discharge ignites the food sample. What advantages does such a calorimeter have over the one you used?

By the way, you may have noticed a green or brown potato chip when you went to get one from the bag for your experiment. A brown chip has not been "over-fried" or burned by the manufacturer. Rather a brown chip comes from a potato that contains more sugar. The more sugar in a chip, the browner it gets when it is fried. A green chip is from a potato that has been exposed to the sun. Normally, potatoes grow underground. But strong winds and heavy rains can erode the soil, exposing a potato to the sun. Like all plants, a potato will produce the green pigment chlorophyll when exposed to sunlight.

Project Idea

Reducing Calories Without Affecting the Taste

One of the major problems facing the snack-food industry has always been how to make a product that is nutritious, nonfattening, and tasty. After years of research, an artificial chemical compound called Olestra, known commercially as Olean, was developed. Olean is the first synthetic food nutrient approved for use by the Food and Drug Administration in more than twenty years. Tests have shown that very few people can tell the difference between regular potato chips and those containing Olean. Chips with Olean, however, contain half the calories as regular chips. Moreover, Olean chips do not have any fat.

Check the Internet for information about Olean. How is it made? What side effects have people experienced after eating potato chips made with Olean?

Experiment 5.2

What Makes Popcorn Pop?

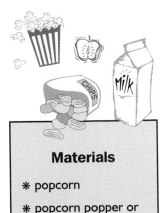

When you hear the word *popcorn*, you probably think of the movies. As soon as you walk into the theater, you can smell the popcorn and even hear it popping. It is almost impossible to pass by the refreshment counter without buying some popcorn before you take your seat. Even if you do, you will probably change

Materials

* popcorn

* popcorn popper or microwave

* sharp knife

* kitchen scale

* an adult

your mind when you see someone else eating popcorn. But with all the popcorn you have probably eaten, have you ever stopped to wonder why it pops? Here is your chance to learn why.

Record the mass of the popcorn before it is popped. If you do not have a popper, use popcorn that can be microwaved. Pop the popcorn and then weigh it again. If you use microwave popcorn, cut open the bag after popping, and allow it to cool before weighing. Compare the masses before and after popping.

Ask an adult to cut some popcorn kernels longitudinally and some horizontally, as shown in Figure 25. If cutting the kernels horizontally is difficult, just cut off the bottom tips. Pop the two different types of cut kernels separately and observe what happens.

Unpopped popcorn kernels contain water. Why does popcorn weigh less after it is popped? What is in the popcorn

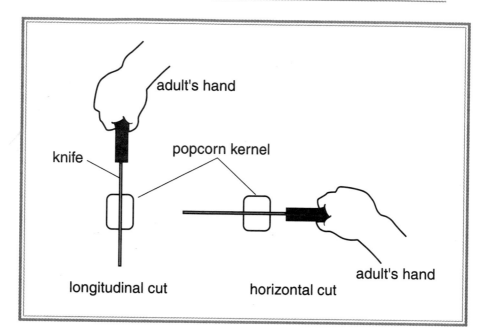

Figure 25. To cut a popcorn kernel longitudinally, **ask an adult** to cut it from top to bottom. To cut it horizontally, cut it from side to side.

that is lost because of heating? You learned in Chapter 1 that water can exist as a solid, liquid, or gas. What state is present in an unpopped kernel? A popped kernel? Why does popcorn expand when it is popped? Explain why the kernels that were cut longitudinally did not pop.

Experiment 5.3

How Can You Make Popcorn "Dance"?

Pop some popcorn. Fill a glass with water. Add 1 tablespoon of baking soda and a few drops of food coloring. Stir well until everything is dissolved. Drop in the popcorn. Pour in 3 tablespoons of vinegar and stir gently. Observe what happens.

Materials
* popcorn
* large, clear drinking glass
* water
* tablespoon
* baking soda
* food coloring
* vinegar

What happened when you added the vinegar? The tiny bubbles that were formed were filled with carbon dioxide gas. This gas is produced when baking soda reacts with vinegar. If the gas bubbles are trapped by the popcorn, the kernels "dance" to the surface. When the bubbles burst at the surface, the kernels "dance" their way back to the bottom. They can continue "dancing" as long as they trap and then release the gas bubbles.

Project Idea

The Water Content of Various Popcorn Brands

Compare different brands of popcorn for their water content. Weigh the popcorn both before and after popping. The difference represents the mass of water that is lost. Divide this mass by the mass of the popcorn before popping, multiply by 100, and you will get the percentage of water in the popcorn. Check to see whether your results depend on the quantity of popcorn kernels you use. In other words, does it matter if you pop all the kernels at once? Test this with 100 kernels that you pop all at once. Then conduct five separate trials, each with 20 kernels. How do the results compare? What happens if you soak the popcorn in water before popping? Soak some kernels for one hour and others overnight. Allow them to dry before popping. Compare their water content and how well they pop. Use a computer spreadsheet to summarize your results.

Experiment 5.4

How Much Sugar Does a Cookie Contain?

A common dessert for lunch at school consists of milk and cookies. So you should not have any trouble getting a variety of cookies to use in this next experiment. But then again, your friends are not likely to give up their cookies unless you are very persuasive. Tell them that their cookies will be put to good use. Inform them that you need the cookies to tell which brand contains the least amount of sugar and thus is less likely to cause cavities.

Materials

* yeast
* measuring cup
* tablespoon
* teaspoon
* 6 small plastic freezer bags
* water
* sugar
* flour
* cookies
* marking pen

Use a marker to number six plastic freezer bags. Place 1 tablespoon of yeast and ¼ cup of water in freezer bag #1. Stand the bag upright so that the contents do not spill but do not seal the bag. Do the same to five other bags. Bag #1 will serve as the control.

Add ¼ teaspoon of sugar to bag #2, ½ teaspoon of sugar to bag #3, and 1 teaspoon of sugar to bag #4. Add 1 tablespoon of flour to bag #5. Gently crush a cookie into small pieces and add 1 tablespoon to bag #6. Check each bag against Figure 26, which shows what should be in each bag.

Squeeze out all the air from each bag and seal. Mix the contents thoroughly. Allow the bags to remain undisturbed for 30 minutes. Observe what happens.

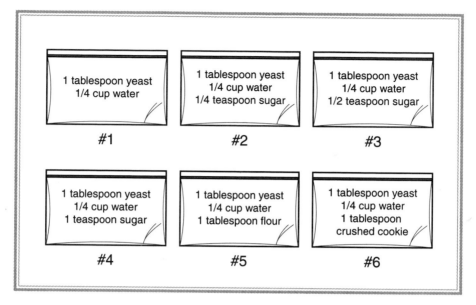

Figure 26. Check your bags against the bags shown here to be sure that you have placed the correct ingredients in each bag.

The sugar reacts with an enzyme supplied by the yeast. The reaction produces carbon dioxide gas, which inflates the freezer bag. The more carbon dioxide produced, the bigger the bag gets. By comparing the size of the bag with the crushed cookie to those containing sugar, you can estimate how much sugar is present in 1 tablespoon of crushed cookie. You can test as many different brands of cookies as you want, depending on how convincing you were to your lunchtime friends. By the way, why did you crush the cookie? Think back to what you did with the liver in Experiment 4.1.

Experiment 5.5

How Much Sugar Does Gum Contain?

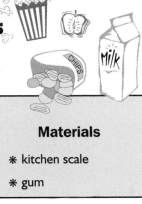

Weigh a piece of gum in its wrapper. Take the gum out of its wrapper and chew. Do not throw away the wrapper. Keep chewing until the gum loses all its taste. Then remove the

Materials

∗ kitchen scale

∗ gum

gum from your mouth, trying to minimize the amount of saliva that is on the gum. Put the chewed gum back in its wrapper and weigh.

Subtract the weight of the chewed gum from the weight of the unchewed gum. As you chewed, the sugar in the gum dissolved in your saliva. Thus the loss in weight represents the mass of sugar that was in the gum. Calculate the percent of sugar in the gum by placing your data in the following equation.

$$\frac{\text{mass of sugar}}{\text{mass of gum}} \times 100 = \text{percent sugar}$$

Keep in mind that you added some saliva to the gum while you were chewing it. Thus the loss in weight after chewing the gum is not as much as it should be. As a result, the percent sugar in the gum should be even higher than your calculation shows. Do some brands of gum contain more sugar than others? Are sugarless gums really sugarless?

Experiment 5.6

What Is Rock Candy?

Sugars are the body's main source of energy. Whenever you need energy, your body processes sugar through a series of chemical reactions. Your body can process other nutrients, including both fats and proteins, but sugars, which are carbohydrates, are the easiest and fastest to use. Thus when you need a quick burst of energy, eat a candy bar or a piece of fruit. But if you are planning to do something tomorrow that will take a large amount of energy, then you should eat pasta or some other food that is high in complex carbohydrates. By tomorrow, the complex carbohydrates will be broken down

Materials

* small pot
* measuring cup
* jar made of thick glass
* wooden spoon
* water
* sugar
* food coloring
* pencil
* string
* scissors
* small plastic button
* plastic wrap
* an adult

into simpler sugars. These sugars will then be available for your body to process for energy. If you do not have any candy bars around the house, here is a simple way to make your own "energy source."

Be sure that a glass jar and button are clean. You can use a canning, jelly, or peanut butter jar. Cut a piece of string slightly longer than the height of the glass jar. Tie one end of the string to a pencil and the other end to the button. The string should be long enough so that the button is close but not touching the bottom of the glass when you assemble everything, as shown in Figure 27. Once you are satisfied with your setup, remove the pencil, string, and button from the jar and set it aside.

Pour 1 cup of water into a pot. Add 2½ cups of sugar and some food coloring to the water. **Under adult supervision,** begin heating the water. Stir the solution with a wooden spoon

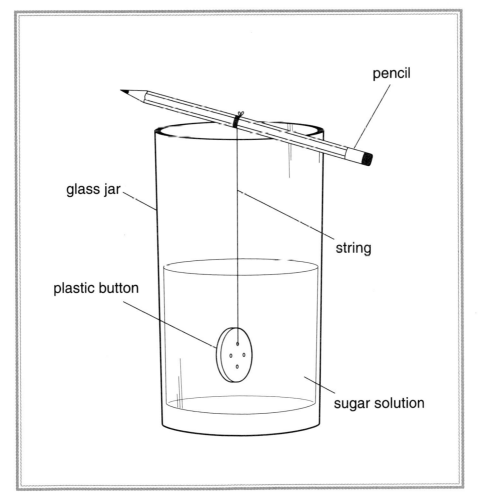

Figure 27. Place the string in the jar after the adult has poured in the hot sugar solution. Sugar will form crystals on the button as the solution slowly cools.

until it boils. Not all the sugar will dissolve until the water is boiling. When it starts to boil, stop stirring. Turn down the heat so that the solution boils gently. Continue to boil for three to four minutes. Turn off the heat.

Ask an adult to pour the hot sugar solution into the glass jar. Place the string in the jar after the solution has been poured into the jar. Lay the pencil over the jar so that the button is dangling in the sugar solution.

When the solution is cool enough to touch, carefully move the jar to a place where it can be left undisturbed for several days. If anyone moves the jar after it has cooled, the experiment will be spoiled. Cover the jar with plastic wrap. Look for sugar crystals that start to form on the button. Remove the string after chunks of sugar crystals have formed. You now have rock candy, which you can eat whenever you need a quick burst of energy.

As heat is applied, the water particles move apart, making more room for the sugar to dissolve. At this point, the solution is said to be supersaturated. A **supersaturated solution** is one that contains more solutes than it normally does at a lower temperature. As a supersaturated solution cools, the solutes start to come out of solution. How is a supersaturated solution involved in making a gelatin dessert?

In this experiment, the sugar forms crystals that collect on the button. The button acts as a "seed" on which the crystals can start growing. If the entire sugar solution turns into one solid mass, then you may have cooled it too long before you poured it into the glass, or you may have stirred it while it was boiling.

Project Idea

Growing Crystals

You may have seen a science kit that is sold for growing crystals. As you have just learned, however, growing crystals can be easily done without a kit. Check your school library or the Internet for information on growing crystals. Experiments have been performed on the space shuttle to see how crystals would grow in zero gravity. Carry out a project that investigates some aspect of crystal growth. As part of your project, use a computer graphics program to simulate the growth of a crystal.

Experiment 5.7

How Many Colors Are Really Present in a Candy?

Sugar-coated candies come in a variety of colors, including red, brown, yellow, orange, blue, and green. But is each color the result of adding a single dye to the sugar coating, or is each color a mixture of different dyes? You can answer this question by carrying out this experiment, which involves chromatography. Recall that chromatography can be used to separate the components that may be present in a liquid or gas. For example, chromatography was used in Experiment 3.5 to separate the various pigments that together make up the green color of spinach. Here you will have the chance to determine which colors used to coat candies are a mixture of different pigments.

Materials

* sugar-coated candies
* white vinegar
* household ammonia
* white woolen yarn
* chromatography paper
* paper towel
* toothpicks
* metric ruler
* four test tubes
* measuring cup
* pot
* water
* stove
* drinking glass
* aluminum foil
* an adult

Cut a 15-cm length of white woolen yarn. The yarn must be 100 percent wool. Place the yarn in a test tube and add 15 mL of white vinegar. **Under adult supervision**, heat the test tube in a pot of boiling water for 5 minutes. Heating the wool in vinegar removes any chemicals from the yarn that may interfere with the separation of the pigments in the candy. After the test tube has cooled, remove the yarn from the vinegar and let it dry on a sheet of paper towel.

Place six sugar-coated candies of the same color in a test tube. Cover them with white vinegar. **Under adult supervision**, heat the test tube in a pot of boiling water until the sugar coatings dissolve. Do not heat the candies for too long because you do not want to dissolve the inside of the candies. After the test tube has cooled, carefully pour the solution into another test tube. Be careful not to transfer any of the solid material.

The solution contains a mixture of different chemicals, including the dyes used to color the candies. To remove just the dyes, add the wool yarn that you heated in vinegar to the test tube. Then add 5 mL of vinegar and heat the test tube in the pot of boiling water for 5 minutes. Heating the test tube will transfer just the dyes from the solution to the yarn. Allow the test tube to cool and remove the yarn.

To release the dyes from the yarn, place it in a clean test tube that contains 10 mL of household ammonia. Gently shake the test tube to mix the yarn and ammonia. Heat the test tube in the pot of boiling water for 5 minutes. Heating the solution will extract the dyes from the yarn and transfer them to the ammonia. Continue heating the test tube to concentrate the solution with the dyes. You can tell the solution is concentrated when it has a dark color.

Follow the procedure outlined in Experiment 3.5 to apply the dye solution to the chromatography paper, as shown in Figure 28. Prepare two strips of chromatography paper with the same dye solution. Pour 5 mL of vinegar into a small

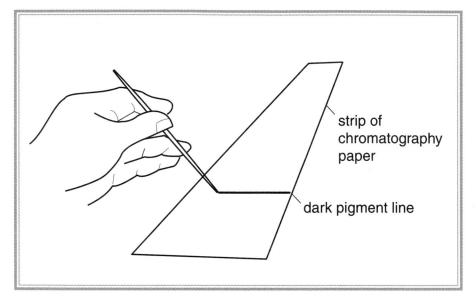

strip of
chromatography
paper

dark pigment line

Figure 28. Be sure to allow each application of pigment solution to dry thoroughly before applying the next one. Make the pigment line as thin and dark as possible.

drinking glass and suspend one of the strips in the solution. Pour 5 mL of household ammonia to suspend the second strip. Cover both glasses with aluminum foil and allow the vinegar to move up the paper strips until it is about 1 cm from the top. Remove the paper strips from the glasses, allow them to dry on a piece of paper towel, and observe what colors are present. Vinegar separates the yellow and blue dyes better, whereas the household ammonia separates the red and yellow dyes better.

Glossary

acid—Chemical whose solution has a pH value less than 7.

anemia—Condition in which the blood does not have enough red blood cells.

atom—Basic unit of matter.

base—Chemical whose solution has a pH value greater than 7.

calorie—Quantity of energy needed to raise the temperature of 1 g of water 1°C.

carbohydrate—Organic compound in which the ratio of carbon, hydrogen, and oxygen ratio is 1:2:1.

cell membrane—Structure that encloses and surrounds a cell.

cell wall—Rigid structure that surrounds the cell membrane of plant cells.

chemical bond—Force that holds two atoms together.

chemical formula—Shorthand method to show the elements and the number of atoms of each that are present in a chemical compound.

chromatography—Process used to separate the various components in a mixture, such as the pigments in a solution.

colligative property—Property that depends on the number of particles present and not on their size or weight.

colloid—Mixture in which one substance is suspended, but not dissolved, in another substance.

control—Experimental design that allows only one factor to determine the results.

density—Quantity of mass present in a given volume.

dependent variable—Factor in an experiment that changes as a result of what the experimenter does.

element—Building block of a chemical compound.

emulsifier—Substance that is used to mix two substances that normally do not mix, like oil and water.

emulsion—Mixture made up of two substances that normally do not mix.

enzyme—Chemical compound that speeds up the rate of a chemical reaction.

filtrate—Liquid that passes through a filter.

hydroponics—Process of growing plants without soil.

independent variable—Factor that the experimenter is free to add or change as part of the procedure.

indicator—Pigment that changes color, depending on the pH of the solution.

lipid—Organic compound that has a high proportion of carbon and hydrogen relative to oxygen.

manometer—Device for measuring the pressure exerted by a liquid or a gas.

microbiology—Study of microscopic organisms such as bacteria.

nonpolar compound—Compound that does not have regions with different electric charges.

organic compound—Compound that contains the element carbon, usually in combination with hydrogen and oxygen.

osteoporosis—Disease in which the bones are brittle and break easily.

ovary—Female reproductive structure in which egg cells are produced.

ovule—Special type of cell that forms inside the ovary of a plant.

pH—Value between 0 and 14 that reflects the acidity of a solution.

photosynthesis—Process by which plants convert carbon dioxide and water into oxygen and sugar.

pigment—Chemical that has a characteristic color.

polar compound—Compound that has regions with different electric charges.

protein—Organic compound that contains the element nitrogen.

qualitative observation—Observation that does not involve making any measurements.

quantitative observation—Observation that involves making a measurement or recording numerical data.

red marrow—Bone marrow with a reddish color because it is the site where red blood cells are produced.

saturated fat—Fat where all the bonds between carbon atoms are single bonds.

seed—Structure produced when a sperm cell fertilizes an egg cell inside the ovule of a plant.

solute—Substance that is dissolved to produce a solution.

solution—Mixture that is prepared by dissolving a solute in a solvent.

solvent—Substance that does the dissolving to produce a solution.

structural formula—Shorthand method used to show the arrangement of all the atoms in a compound.

supersaturated solution—Solution that contains more solutes than it normally does under a given set of conditions.

trichinosis—Disease caused by a roundworm that is found in contaminated meats, especially pork.

turgor pressure—Internal pressure created by water pushing on the cell membrane of a plant cell.

unsaturated fat—Fat that contains one or more double bonds between carbon atoms.

variable—Factor that can change during an experiment.

yellow marrow—Bone marrow that has a yellowish color because it is the site where fats are stored.

Further Reading

Books

Bochinski, Julianne Blair. *The Complete Handbook of Science Fair Projects*. New York: John Wiley and Sons, 1996.

Buckbee, Susan, et al. *Incredible Edibles: Science You Can Eat!* Akron, Ohio: National Convention Center, 1996.

D'Amico, Joan, and Karen E. Drummond. *The Science Chef: 100 Fun Food Experiments & Recipes for Kids*. New York: John Wiley and Sons, 1995.

Gardner, Robert. *Science Projects About the Human Body*. Springfield, N.J.: Enslow Publishers, Inc., 1993.

———. *Science Projects About Kitchen Chemistry*. Springfield, N.J.: Enslow Publishers, Inc., 1999.

Herbert, Don. *Mr. Wizard's Supermarket Science*. New York: Random House, 1980.

Lewis, James. *Hocus Pocus Stir and Cook: The Kitchen Science Magic Book*. New York: Meadowbrook Press, 1991.

Newton, David. *Science—Technology—Society Projects for Young Scientists*. Danbury, Conn.: Franklin Watts, Inc., 1991.

Tocci, Salvatore. *How to Do a Science Fair Project*. Danbury, Conn.: Franklin Watts, Inc., 1997.

Internet Addresses

American Chemical Society. *ACSWeb*. 1998–1999. <http://www.acs.org/> (March 4, 1999).
The society publishes a magazine called ChemMatters, *which focuses on the fun and practical applications of chemistry.*

FDA. "Overview." *Center for Food Safety & Applied Nutrition.* March 2, 1999. <http://vm.cfsan.fda.gov/list.html> (March 4, 1999).
This site has information about foods and government regulations affecting the food industry.

FNIC/NAL/USDA. *Food and Nutrition Information Center.* n.d. <http://www.nal.usda.gov/fnic/> (March 4, 1999).
Sections on this site include food safety, food composition, and healthful school meals.

————. "Food and Nutrition Science Fair Project Resource List." *General Resources.* May 1996. <http://www.nal.usda.gov/fnic/pubs/bibs/gen/scifbr.htm> (March 4, 1999).
This site has a science fair project resource list that includes books and links to other Web sites.

Hands On Science Outreach. n.d. <http://www.hands-on-science.org/> (March 4, 1999).
One section is devoted to "Kids" with information on things to do at home and an opportunity to provide feedback.

Numerous colleges and universities offer programs in food science. Use a search engine to locate their Web sites by typing in the key words *food science.*

List of Suppliers

Scientific supply companies usually sell their merchandise only to schools and not to individuals. Thus, you may need to check with your science teacher if you need a chemical or special piece of glassware that is not available at home. Your school may have the item that you need. If not, ask your teacher for a catalog from one of these companies. By looking through the catalog, you may get ideas on how to come up with your own substitute for a piece of equipment or glassware that is not only cheaper but also reflects your creativity. This will not only help you to carry out your project, but will also serve to impress anyone who takes the time to look at it. Two companies where you can order supplies directly and have them mailed to your home are

Edmund Scientific
101 E. Gloucester Pike
Barrington, NJ 08007
1-609-573-6250
1-609-547-3488

Educational Innovations, Inc.
151 River Road
Cos Cob, CT 06807-2514
http://www.teachersource.com

Index

A

acids
  definition, 58
  examples, 61
  precipitation, 60–61, 62, 63
aspirin, 57, 58
atoms, 6, 17, 42, 43, 44, 46, 48

B

bacteria, 93–95
bases
  definition, 58
  examples, 61
bones, 92, 93
butter, 33, 42–44, 48–50, 51

C

cake decorating, 56
calories
  definition, 98–99
  in potato chips, 100, 102–104
candy, 116–118
carbohydrates, 77
carbon dioxide, 29, 107, 110
cheese, 34–36
chemical
  bond, 44, 48–49
  definition, 6
  formula, 6, 43
  structural formula, 43–44, 47
cholesterol, 42, 44
chromatography
  definition, 70
  experiment, 67, 69, 116–118

colligative property, 20, 21
colloid, 32–33, 34
control, 7–8
crystals, 115

D

density, 16
diets, 50, 100–104
dyes, 55, 56–57, 59, 116

E

element, 42
emulsifier, 53–54
emulsion, 53
enzymes, 77, 78, 110
  in liver, 80–82

F

fats, 42–44, 50, 86, 88, 89–90
  saturated and unsaturated, 44,
    46–50
fruit, 23–25

G

gelatin, 77–78

H

hydrogenation, 48
hydroponics, 76

I

ice cream, 21
iron in food, 83–84
irradiated foods, 97

L

lipids, 42–43
liver, 80–82

M

margarine, 42, 48, 49–50
mass vs. weight, 40
mayonnaise, 53
meat tenderizer, 85
microbiology, 94
minerals in milk, 38–40

O

observations
    qualitative vs. quantitative, 44–45
oils, 42–44, 46, 47, 49, 53
organic compound, 42, 57, 77
    polar vs. nonpolar, 47
osteoporosis, 93

P

pH, 60–61
photosynthesis
    definition, 64
    experiment, 64–66
pigments
    definition, 55
    indicators, 59
    in plants, 67, 69
plants
    experiments, 64–66, 67, 69, 71–72
    seeds, 74–75
popcorn, 105–106, 107
potato chips, 100–104
project ideas, 21, 28, 37, 41, 50, 63, 70, 73, 76, 83–84, 89–90, 91, 93–95, 97, 104, 108, 115
proteins
    chemical composition, 77
    in milk, 38, 41–42

R

red cabbage, 59–60
rock candy, 112–114

S

safety advice, 8–9, 58
salt, 6, 18, 20
scientific models, 15–16
seeds, 74–75
soda, 29
solute, 22, 23, 24, 29–30, 31, 34, 38
solutions, 22, 26, 32
    supersaturated, 114
solvent, 22, 23, 30, 31, 47, 89
sugar content in food, 109–111

T

temperature scales, 16–17
trichinosis, 96
turgor pressure, 71–72, 73

V

variables, dependent and independent, 8
vitamin C, 24–28

W

water, 6, 11–12, 13–14, 15–16, 22
    boiling point, 16
    freezing point, 16, 18, 20